D0910233

CHEWED WATER

Chewed Water

A   M E M O I R

Aishah Rahman

aka Virginia Hughes

University Press of New England

Hanover and London

Published by University Press of New England, Hanover, NH 03755

© 2001 by Aishah Rahman

All rights reserved

Printed in the United States of America

5 4 3 2 1

From *The Collected Poems of Langston Hughes* by Langston Hughes, copyright © 1994 by The Estate of Langston Hughes. Used by permission of Alfred A. Knopf, a division of Random House, Inc.

Verses from "House of the Spider" by Angela Jackson, *Open Places* 37 (spring/summer 1984) appear on the part pages of the book.

Library of Congress Cataloging-in-Publication Data

Rahman, Aishah.
    Chewed water : a memoir / by Aishah Rahman aka Virginia Hughes.
        p.cm.
    ISBN 1-58465-143-1 (alk. paper)
    1. Rahman, Aishah. 2. Dramatists, American—20th century—Biography.
3. African American women—New York (State)—New York—Biography. 4. African American families—New York (State)—New York. 5. African American dramatists —Biography. 6. Harlem (New York, N.Y.)—Biography.
    1. Title.
    PS3568.A4135 Z464 2001
    812'.54—DC21   2001003037

For
Yoruba
my daughter

This act of homage tastes bittersweet with memories.

ACKNOWLEDGMENTS

With their art and example, friendship and support, so many people gave me the emotional courage to complete this book. Some of them are Amiri Baraka, Maya Breuer, Nikki Coleman, Donna and Tim Coutis, Virgina Cox, Thadious Davis, Elaine Hughes, Helen Lang, Hettie Jones, Carole Maso, Therese Plair, Teena Potter; Maketa Dorothy White and the folks at D'Zora House, The Barbara Deming Memorial Fund for Women, Yaddo, my colleagues in the Brown University's Creative Writing Program, the women of 640 West, especially Stephanie Berry, Bettye Jiles and Jeanne Nedd, the Sealy family, my agent, Tom D'Evelyn with his gifts of jazz and unwavering faith, Phil Pochoda, and always Yoruba, whose love continually sustains, elevates and inspires.

Jill Nelson

In works of literary fiction situated in the Harlem community, particularly those written after the Harlem Renaissance, what is most often missing are the voices of African American women. This profound and troubling absence is most obvious in literature about Harlem in the 1940s and 1950s, in which women's voices are almost completely unheard as primary voices in the coming of age narrative.

Noted playwright Aishah Rahman's brilliant memoir, *Chewed Water*, the story of a young girl's coming of age in Harlem in the years immediately following World War II and the decade afterward, steps into this void with a voice that is alternately seductive, funny, helpless, raw, angry, active, and passive. What Rahman's voice never is, is quiet. In language rich with the cadences of rhythm and blues, jazz and gospel, *Chewed Water* provides a lyrical, cool, rejuvenating drink of Black women's voices, experiences, and perceptions in this previously male-dominated body of coming-of-age literature. If we didn't before, we now realize what we have been missing because of what Rahman has created. As *Chewed Water* makes beautifully clear, the coming-of-age story has too often been a literary tradition that, when it comes to the silence of Black women's voices and the absence of their stories, might well be described as a wasteland.

This is the story of a black girl's transition into young womanhood in all its glory, pain, and complexity. Virginia Hughes is a foster child, left as an infant with a Caribbean woman in Harlem by her mother, May Anna. May Anna, part of the massive Southern migration to the North that characterized the pre- and post-War years, leaves the South with great hope and courage. A scant few years later she is sick, unable to work, and forced to abandon her only child.

The scene is set. What follows is the mesmerizing story of Virginia's coming of age in a Harlem that fascinates. Rahman's vivid, visual descriptions of church services and street lives, of beatings and the bonding between Virginia and her foster sisters, of teenage dancers eagerly entering the Savoy Ballroom on Saturday afternoons and the crackle of sexual heat that the girl Virginia observes in confusion and that the young woman slowly begins to understand and embrace, bring this female, fecund, forgotten Harlem brilliantly to life. This is a book in which the captured language of memory leaps from the page. In Rahman's deft hands, the voices of southerners, northerners, and islanders wrap around each other, creating the roux that was young Virginia's Harlem community, both cradle and crucible.

Chewed Water is both a celebration and an open-eyed portrait of a particular community in a particular time. It is also the story of Virginia's harrowing journey to young womanhood, a journey in which fear is a tool of guidance. Fear of receiving yet another beating, of "turning out like her mother," of anyone who does not meet the approval of her foster mother, Mrs. Feral, of being trapped—by men, by her own sexuality, by life. This is a memoir of a young girl's fighting to find out not only where she came from and who she is, but, most importantly, who she might become. And true to real life, *Chewed Water* is no one-note song, but a complex literary composition, sometimes hilarious, wrenching, shocking, joyous, soothing, loving and painful, always powerfully and beautifully written, always compelling and revelatory.

The people who populate *Chewed Water* live under Aishah Rahman's hand, as well they should; these are people Rahman knows intimately and who many, many readers will recognize. They are, lovingly and sometimes painfully familiar, characters in our own lives, met along the journey to our own womanhood, perhaps still struggled with as we fight to gain or retain our independence, even full grown. Like the finest of coming-of-age literature, *Chewed Water* is a book to be read and read again. Guaranteed each time a new discovery, whether it is a snippet of information missed before, a precise and unique turn of phrase so beautiful it makes you stop and read it again, or a bit of someone's monologue about southern blacks or West Indians so thick with class, color, and cultural contradictions it'll make you laugh out loud and shake your head in shame.

All praises due to Aishah Rahman for this courageous and beautifully written memoir. Like a haunting jazz riff or gospel chorus, *Chewed Water* resonates long after reading, a blues chorus that we cannot shake. In this memoir, Rahman artfully situates Black women squarely in this place and time, in the coming-of-age narrative, and in the crucial work of self-definition.

my torn house

shivers   in the wind

ragged   edges like

open nerves.

—*Angela Jackson,*
"The House of the Spider"

I

Girlhood to me means 103 West 120th street, apartment #23, my address in Harlem; Mrs. Feral, my foster mother; and that day in March 1956 when, in New York City's Family Court, I relinquished my three-month-old son for adoption. There was no eager adoptive family waiting to take him from my arms that wintry March morning but I signed adoption papers anyway. My fervent hope was that eventually he would be adopted but until that time, Sheltering Arms Children's Service could place him in a foster home as they had done with me eighteen years ago.

I named the squalling infant in my arms Kelvin, because in 1955 I had not yet met anyone with that name and that seemed reason enough to choose it. His middle name was Randolph, after an actor, Randolph Scott, whom I had once seen in the movies. And as was the custom then, because I was a bastard, I bore only my mother's last name and my son would do the same. Kelvin Randolph Hughes.

In the courtroom, on that bitter morning when winter stung with ice, I was accompanied by the only adult with whom I ever had a truthful conversation, my social worker, Mrs. Wallings. In her office she would lean toward me, her round brown eyes glistening with sympathy as she made comforting, clucking sounds and patted my hand, and now she would be the witness to this adoption ritual.

Just a few hours before, as dawn rose frostily and Kelvin cried, one of the nurses at Inwood House tried to dissuade me from giving him away. "You'll be sorry," she said. "Your firstborn? Don't do it. Look at those eyes, that hair, his mouth. You'll never have another like him." But I just continued to feed him and afterward dress him in the mint green crochet layette that Mrs. Walling had contributed especially for the occasion.

At French Hospital, the small hospital on Twenty-Ninth Street, where Inwood girls went to give birth, the white girls, without exception, had their babies taken by eager adoptive families straight from their birth beds; they had the option of never seeing or even knowing the sex of their unwanted newborns. But since Negro adoptive parents preferred the lighter skinned infants, I was forced to linger at Inwood House on 15th Street and Ninth Avenue for three months to take care of Kelvin while I waited for Sheltering Arms to find him a foster home. In those long, dreary days I learned to feed and bathe the creature that had emerged from my body and could not sustain my initial hatred. What I abhorred was that his conception seemed to fulfill Mrs. Feral's evil prophecies.

While my own mother's face is unknown to me, Mrs. Feral's glittering brown eyes, her smooth, firm, glowing, dark skin, her husky voice chanting at me, even in my sleep, just like May Anna, just like May Anna, the whisper of her felt slippers in the morning, her ribbed flannel cloth she wore on her right arthritic knee and her formidable aura of righteousness are very vivid.

Mommi, for that is what I called my foster mother, ran a household that was a citadel of religion, rigidity, and discipline against the encroaching evils of Harlem. A short, solidly built, compact woman, Mrs. Feral wielded a fierce moral authority that none dared defy. Except me.

My eighteen years of life had been spent as an asteroid orbiting around her, and living in her volatile atmosphere made me an accurate forecaster of Mommi's weather. Usually she began her mornings with a saturnine calm toward me. By noon her sky would have already turned dark, heralding a hailstorm of words soon followed by an eruption of the angry lava that boiled near her surface and exploded into volcanic thuds upon my head. In the evening, spent and exhausted, I knew her mood would ease down to a glacial frost while in my room I prayed to May Anna to come and rescue me.

Although we had just arrived in the courtroom, I was already impatient. Where was the judge? I wanted to get this over with and leave the courtroom forever, yet dreaded the coming moments. Kelvin began to whimper and break the cavernous silence as the three of us waited for the judge and his clerks to appear. However, it was not his voice that I heard.

2

"Nothing from nothing leaves nothing. Can't make a silk purse out of a sow's ear. Your own mother didn't want you! She dropped you like a turd so how dare you defy me when I'm only trying to make something decent out of you?"

Now gargoyles with stinging tails burst from her mouth. As they stream toward me her demonic words deafen me, their huge fists bloody my brain, their hateful sound curls tightly around my heart, making it difficult to breathe. I dare not take my eyes away from her hands. The right hand curls around the snake in her apron pocket while a finger on the left one points at me. The skin on her hands is firm and glowing, smooth and velvet brown like the cocoa in her favorite cup. Those hands slap me and burn across my face. They leave their imprint on my cheek and make my head swivel.

"One more time. What are you hiding inside that book?" Nothing, I lie. One of the slaps I received this week was when she raided my room and found my secret trove of comic books. She ripped up the twenty-three *Wonder Woman*s, fifteen *Captain Marvel*s, and twelve *Batman and Robin*s that I planned to trade with Fat Helen.

"A hard head makes a soft ass."

To save myself I could tell her the truth but something inside of me won't let me speak and instead I stare stonily past her.

Outside, Fat Helen, Renee, and Rosie and Lilly Armstrong jump rope. In my head, I jump up and down, swing my hips from left to right and chant along with them as their voices float through the open window:

Jelly in a dish
Makes me sick
A wiggle waggle
Wiggle waggle
Two, four, six.

Yellow Eric, Scoophead Johnson, and Liver Lips are playing stickball, their torrents of laughter rising from the asphalt. From the large Philco emerges Walter Winchell's strident staccato as he informs Mr. and Mrs. America of Josephine Baker's audacious demand to be served at the exclusive Stork Club. All the sounds recede into the background as Mommi continues, "Annnd when I finish with you, your ass is going to be softer than a loaded baby diaper!"

I want to laugh but I am terrified and too angry.

"Bring those dirty, filthy, trashy, comic books to me!"

I glance at the neatly arranged *Readers Digests, Ebony Magazines, Daily News, Amsterdam News,* a red, leather-covered Church of England hymnal next to the King James Version of the Bible on one shelf, and on a shelf underneath, Sinclair Lewis's *Kingsblood Royal* and Joseph Scott Barrie's *Little Minister.* The next three of the five shelves of the household bookcase were empty. She never even read *Wonder Woman.* She just thinks comic books are dirty because I like them. Besides, after having my face slapped at unpredictable times all week long, she's crazy if she thinks I'll go anywhere near her. She's crazy if she thinks I'll deliver my precious comic book so she can tear it up with one hand and slap me with the other. Absolutely not. I can't let her see it. I won't move.

Now, the room hums with her silence. Everyone is looking at me except Daddy, who has buried his head deeper in his newspaper.

Seconds pass and I know each one brings me nearer to the coiled cord in her pocket. The ringing children's voices are gone. The glow from the streetlamp light has replaced the rose-filtered sunset. Walter Winchell's voice has disintegrated to a faint static buzz. An iridescent green beetle invades the room, scuttles along the window, and escapes to the outside. The smell of frying chicken wafts into the room as downstairs, Fat Helen's mother begins to cook dinner.

Mommi is becoming a cyclone. I know the signs. Any moment she will lunge, puffed up with anger, spiraling crazily toward me, slashing left and right as her iron cord snakes through the air, knocking down chairs and destroying anything in her path, only intent on demolishing me. I've got her so exactly timed that the moment before she springs for me, I shuffle toward her. Sick and elated at my victory of making her move first, I now inch toward her, clutching *Wonder Woman* in my hands, whimpering with every half step. She is waiting to whip me, for loving comic books, to whip me for lying. A few feet from her I stop, not daring to enter the circle of electricity that crackles around her. I dream about having magic bracelets on each wrist to repel whatever blows she sends my way. The bulge of the iron cord in her apron pocket enrages me and suddenly I rip Wonder Woman in colorful shreds that flutter to the floor.

THWAP! Aunt Syl, Daddy, Rose, and Teddie scatter as the thick cord springs from her pocket and whips through the air and connects to my flesh. BAM! As Mommi chases me, I knock over chairs and crawl under the table trying to escape. She pins me down and, yelping with pain and fury, I plot and scheme under the rain of blows. "I'll find you May Anna. Soon as I'm old enough I'll run away and I'll find you somewhere." On the floor, on my knees, I scuttle every direction. I shield my face from the rope with my hands and OOUAWAHHH! blood leaks from my fingertips. My knees, legs, and arms are crisscrossed with welts. BWAM! Again there is a thud across my back and buttocks. I am crisscrossed with rising welts. Every inch of flesh stings. Open cuts dot my legs, arms, and face. And then the storm is over. It is time for her to cook dinner, indeed, she is late. Now she moves around in her kitchen, from time to time looking up to God through the kitchen ceiling as she sings.

> I know that my redeemer liveth
> And because he lives,
> And because he lives.
> I too, I tooo
> Shall liiiive.

All the while I am in my room sobbing and talking to May Anna as I always did in the afterthrobs, in the blood of bruises, in the rising of new welts, in the stinging, swollen flesh, my hot sobbing tears splashing down on keloids of old wounds on aching purple blood clots on blood seeping out of bloody mashed fingertips tasting bland tasteless blood in slit lips in rising, broken flesh, blood bruises sobbing, throbbing bruises open bloody sobbing flesh in purple clotted throbbing finger nails sobbing one word. Mother.

—

"You all right?" asks Teddie, hours later, lying on her bottom bunk in our room.

"Leave me alone."

"Why?"

"You told on me."

"I had to."

"You did not."

"Did too."

"Why?"

"Cause."

"Cause why?"

"I'm not like you. I'm afraid of beatings."

"So am I."

"Not like me. I'm really scared."

"You still didn't have to tell. You didn't have to show her."

"That's what you think . . . are we still sisters?"

"No!"

"Awww Gin-gin!"

"Wait till you get a beating. I'm going to laugh at you."

"I don't get beatings."

"That's because you're a sneak."

"I am not. I just don't get 'em."

"That's because you got a mother."

"Do not. Muriel is supposed to be my aunt, right?"

"Right."

"Besides, I didn't laugh at you."

"Did too, I saw you, I heard you. Just wait."

"I didn't mean to. Honest. If I give you something can we be sisters again?"

"Maybe. Lemme see."

Teddie rises from her bed and tiptoes to our bureau. Opening a drawer she pulls out something and offers it to me. It is a photograph of all of us on a summer's day. Mommi and Aunt Syl are wearing cotton sun dresses and straw hats. Daddy has on blue suspenders and a felt hat even though it is summertime. Sixteen-year-old Rose has her hair in a pageboy and wears very carefully applied lipstick. Teddie's big round eyes stare directly in the camera. We are at Bear Mountain State Park and have just finished a picnic lunch. In the photograph are the wicker baskets filled with fried chicken, codfish cakes, cassava pie, potato salad, and deviled eggs. A big jug of Mommi's delicious lemonade is on the ground beside a black cast-iron pot of peas and rice. Everyone is feeling loose and our faces are relaxed and smiling. Everyone except Aunt Syl, whose smile is not an expression of joy but a grimace of endurance as if she is looking at the long span of lonely years looming before her. And I, imitating a model's pose, have my hands on my bony hips and my flat chest thrust forward, imitating *Lena* Horne's pouty smile. My thick, shoulder-length hair is straightened, black and shiny, with curls at the end. I have on my favorite white pinafore dress and red Mary Jane shoes. I think I am cute. Looking at this photograph always made me happy. But now with my body stinging I feel ashamed. What is inside of me that makes me rebel? Maybe Mommi is right and I have inherited bad blood. Why does it hurt when she curses May Anna who is only a faceless stranger? Why doesn't May Anna come and see about me? Has she forgotten that I was born? My mother is an example of what happens to girls who do it before marriage. I would rather die than repeat her sin, the sin of doing it before marriage, becoming pregnant and dumping a baby on a stranger.

"Here," I say, handing Teddie back her picture. "You keep it, it's yours. I don't like the way I look in it anyhow."

It was August 15, 1946, and in my room I wondered where May Anna was. Did she see the green light in the sky that came just before sunrise? Or the raindrops that glistened in the sunshine on 14th Street? On Fifth Avenue parasols became umbrellas in a sudden downpour. In Central Park sunbathers were treated to cooling rain showers. On 42nd Street the sunshine was bright as the rain poured down only on one side of the street. When it rains in the sunshine it's just the Devil beating his wife, laughed folks on 120th Street, and I wondered why doesn't the sun eclipse, refuse to shine and pitch the world into darkness until the satanic violence stops? And in apartment #23 where all of us were extensions of the weather inside of us, there were hurricanes, floods, thick fog, and scattered sunshine.

3

Finally, the judge enters the courtroom, behind him, his two clerks. His clerks are also middle-aged white men. His hair is black, no, grayish black, sparse. I cannot see his eyes; he does not even glance my way. Kelvin begins to wail again; I am not breathing. In his seat, the judge looms down before us. On his desk, stacks of paper, a brown thick book with pages edged in dull gold. He opens it and shuts it almost at once. He opens it again. The clerks move back and forth. They hand the judge more papers. Kelvin continues to cry. I cannot keep his bottle steady in my shaking hands. Miss Walling leans over and murmurs, easy now, there's a long wait ahead.

I will wait. I have a strong belief in tomorrow. Tomorrow will come. Tomorrow will be better. The future is already looking brighter, I think, since Kelvin's possibility of adoption is an upward move since I had only been a foster child. With luck, he will be more than someone's monthly check.

4

They needed each other but that didn't make the two women friends. On the day May Anna first brought me to 120th Street in 1938, Mrs. Feral's shapeless build and immaculate cotton house dress made her self-conscious of her tight skirt and ample buttocks. "You Americans," Mrs. Feral said in an accent that was new to May Anna. "We work hard to get someplace, we stick close in our family. You Americans have a different kind of breeding, I guess."

Anger warmed May Anna. She glanced around the plastic-covered furniture and lace doilies. Seditty monkey chaser. Banana eater. Black Jew, she thought, but held her tongue because she needed this woman and besides she did not want to cough.

"What about your people in North Carolina. Do they know about Virginia?" "They dead," lied May Anna. Well it was almost true. All the men were dead or gone away. Most of the women, in her family from generation to generation, alone. That's what she was trying to escape, what seemed to her eyes as the black curse: death for the men; aloneness for the women. My mother believed she could leave it behind but that day, standing, facing Mrs. Feral in her living room, she must have felt that the curse was slowly creeping up on her.

May Anna remembered how in 1930, one April morning, she looked at her mother and finally felt courageous enough to declare, I got my ticket Ma, I'm gone to New York.

Yula sucked on her lower lip and kept on carving the letters May Anna had taught her. She loved the feel and the smell of the pine wood in her hands, the way the letters were born under her knife. Her father had showed her how to whittle, and now with May Anna standing before her she thought of her father's hands, his long slim fingers that played a banjo and held a harmonica, fingers that flew in the air as graceful birds whenever he spoke and that were smashed to pulp as he died in the red gutters of Wilmington, 1898. She looked at May Anna and thought how much her daughter favored the grandfather she had never seen and then she started rambling about how they had been moving all over for a long time and how they came to be in Wilmington, a litany May Anna had heard many times before and did not want to hear again at that moment.

"None of us ever run from the South. Even your Grandaddy, Jordan. One time though he planned to. Planned to get out after 'mancipation just like everybody else and head toward Kansas. But your Grandaddy's sap ran high so he joined a secret society instead." Yula paused, sucking on a wad of tobacco and examining the wood in her hands, which she planned to whittle into the word, L I V E.

"It was so secret it didn't have no name or no members. They just wanted to see if there was any Southern state where us could get a living and enjoy rights. They worked from state to state, every place where us had been slaves. Your Grandaddy worked in the fields, everywhere to see what sort of living our people lived. About one hundred and fifty men traveled in that way to get the truth of our condition first hand. They passed word along about the true condition of our race. Oh there were some places where Negroes were not being cheated or whipped, some places that from time to time tried to pay what they had promised. Papa's report was simple, 'The general state of things in the South is that nothing is too mean for white folks to do to our people. Get Out!' But in 1888 your grandmother was pregnant with me and so your granddaddy Jordan stayed and was doing good. Too good for some white folks. And you know the rest. The South is our Holy Land. Our Blood make it so." Yula stopped whittling and looked deep into May Anna. "Stop. Don't go. You s'pose to be the black in my gray hair and a firm step in my feebleness."

May Anna looked away, unable to meet her mother's eyes, yet Yula loomed large before her. She saw Yula, a woman born into the world with a good mind and some talent doing the same mule work her grandmother's mother had done.

Since the Civil War her family had graduated from slavery to sharecropping. They were charged 30% on the dollar for the provisions they were rationed. And if any children were caught attending school they could not draw any rations. But she had learned to read and now so had Yula. She saw Yula's worn body now grateful for the invisibility and restfulness of age, weary from tobacco priming and stalk cutting. She saw Yula and other women with a man only from time to time, although there had been plenty birthing, nursing, and burying. Once, May Anna's father came to live with them. Yula cooked him everything she thought he wanted. He would lead Yula to think he wanted something special to eat and when she went to the time and trouble to make it the best she knew how, he would go hungry rather than give her the pleasure of seeing him enjoy what she had made especially for him. Her mother's only comment was that "your father stay mad to keep from getting mad. There's nothing I can do to make him stay."

And now she too was leaving. She was leaving because she could see her life rising up and Yula trying to push it down and strangle it by making her stay.

"Girl, ain't you got no feelings at all?" Yula asked. Automatically May Anna involuntarily pulled her left ear with her left hand as she always did in times of stress. In the right pocket of a seersucker striped blue dress she knew she would never wear again soon as she escaped was a letter that said:

New York is Kingdom Come
Harlem is one big party
Have you got your 1-way yet?
Signed your friend,
Hattie, Jr.

In the left pocket lay twenty-two tobacco-stained dollars, thirty-five bronze-colored, Indian Head pennies; five silver dimes with wings coming out of each side of Liberty's cap; five silver, Liberty-head dollars; ten half-dollar pieces with a flowing-haired Liberty in robes walking in front of a sunrise. Liberty.

Where is the baby's father? Do you even know who he is? May Anna was jolted back to Mrs. Feral's parlor by the woman's questions. May Anna did not lower her eyes or hang her head or mumble. Instead she answered clearly. Me. I'm the baby's father. Anything else you want to know? Mrs. Feral held her tongue. She knew that Sheltering Arms Children's Service was desperate for homes for Negro children but still, she couldn't afford to wait any longer for another placement. Money was tight all over especially in Harlem. And she had dreams. A house in Long Island. Private school for Rose. The things someone of her class should have. Without these credentials folks would mistake her for being like the rest of the low lifers in Harlem. So she looked at the hussy with a coughing toddler and held her tongue.

May Anna, in spite of herself, coughed also as she glared at Mrs. Feral and thought about James Manman Jackson.

―

Welcome to Harlem
Jews own it,
Irish police it,

Negroes have fun in it
Folks from Down South
Welcome to Up South
May Ancestors protect you
Pray that God don't neglect you!

As the brownish red man called Manman (Say it two times so you don't forget) led the toast to her and poured libations on the pulsating wooden floor, a woman floating by said, "Pay him no attention honey, Harlem is heaven!"

Manman laughed as he put his arms around her. "All you singers are alike. Wild happiness or deep misery. I'm telling May Anna like it tis. How it be. The real deal."

"Soon as your suitcases get cold, come around the corner to Connie's Inn. I'm singing on the weekend," said the singer in high liquid voice with a slight drawl before she floated away.

"You must be hungry," Manman said. "Let me buy you a plate," and without waiting for her response he walked away, and she noticed that although his left foot slowly dragged behind the right one his limp did not diminish his erect posture.

"If the oppression don't get you, the Depression will. C'mon children, stomp those blues away," wailed a voice from the Victrola and the bare floorboards shivered with shuffling feet.

"Is ev-e-r-ybody hap-py?" Hattie Jr.'s voice chanted above the music and laughter.

"Yeah mannnnn!" a chorus answered as the top floor rear echoed with music and laughter. It seemed miraculous to May Anna that she was standing in Harlem on a Saturday night in the middle of a rent party. Twelve steps away from Yula out the cabin door, fifteen hundred miles by bus from Wilmington to the village of Harlem, New York, and six flights of narrow, steep winding stairs to Hattie Jr.'s sixth-floor rear kitchenette straight into her first Saturday night function! As she had climbed the six steep flights to Hattie Jr. she had dreamed. Her long fingers would hit typewriter keys instead of bleeding from picking ripe leaves from tobacco stalks that grew six feet tall. Soft suede ankle straps with open toes for her feet would compensate for those hours standing in the cold, red, slimy mud the tobacco leaf grew in. When she finally reached the sixth floor May Anna had knocked on apartment 6D and the door had flown open and Hattie Jr. had screamed, You made it and May Anna stepped into her first New York party. She hardly recognized her old friend whose short hair was shiny black and marcelled with deep waves and whose skin somehow seemed lighter.

"Hey y'all another one from home just got here," Hattie had announced as she pulled May Anna into the packed kitchen and announced, "this ain't just only a rent party no more. It just became May Anna's welcome also."

Manman had immediately claimed her attention. He was at least a shoulder taller than her and a good deal older.

"I just made twenty," she had answered when he had asked her age while refusing to divulge his.

"How old do I look?" he had retorted, knowing she couldn't tell.

And now Manman was returning, bearing an overflowing paper plate with one hand and leading a smiling woman by the other.

"May Anna, meet Cleota Johnson, a Negro business woman with an establishment right here in Harlem," Manman said, handing her the paper plate. The wiry, sweet-smelling, chocolate, round-faced, middle-aged woman threw her arms around May Anna, saying, "You right at home honey. Lots of us from North Carolina live right in this block. Banana eaters live further down on 120th Street round Mount Morris Park and all up and down Lenox Avenue. Folks from Virginia and Georgia settle further up in the 140's but ain't no one but us tar heels all up and down 133rd and Lenox. So you ain't among strangers."

May Anna felt as if she was being initiated into some kind of elite society. Everyone was being so kind, so good. Hattie Jr. exhausted and flushed came up to her saying, "Oh May Anna, I'm so glad I didn't have to come back down to get you. There's plenty folks to meet and plenty to eat and drink. There's homemade corn liquor for 50 cents a shot, and poker and black jack back in the bedroom for those who like to mix gambling with their drinking and dancing. At first I thought rent parties were disgraceful but when I could only make diddly-squat as a domestic, I learned to throw rent-parties just like everyone else."

As May Anna began to get used to these parties she listened hard and learned a lot. She heard about the surge of European immigration and the rise of Fascism in Hattie's packed kitchen. When Roosevelt became governor of New York it was analyzed over bid whist. She cracked up at their dirty jokes about selling pencils and pussy on the corner when Hoover talked to four and one-half million unemployed Americans about self-help instead of government aid. Sometimes she was filled with dread at the state of the world and things she had no control over, but then when the music played, a feeling would reach all the way down to her shoes and May Anna would dance until the cops came to quiet them all down or until it was time for her to take the trolley to the corner of Prospect Avenue and 161st Street in the Bronx and stand in line with the other women on the corner at seven a.m. in an effort to get picked for day work.

━

On her left side stood a woman whose leathery brown face was pinched with age, while on her right a tall skinny girl stood with her little boy, who kept spitting in his hands and rubbing them together in an effort to keep warm. "First thing you should know, any gal I hire has to take a bath . . . and I deduct the time," said a woman in a long fur coat dragging along the sidewalks, walking up and down surveying the morning applicants and stopping in front of May Anna.

"If I could just touch it. It is mink. Or is it sable? Oh I don't know. It gleams in the cold winter sun. The fur is so thick the coat is almost

stiff. It hangs in folded pleats that barely move when you walk up and down looking us over. It smells like powder and perfume. It has no shape. It hangs on you like a rug. Its fur collar brushes your cheeks. Lift up the hem lift up the hem of your coat. If I could just feel with my fingertips don't just let it drag in the streets when I could just touch it and be made warm made radiant warm."

"Can't you hear? I said, hold out your hands and let me see your fingernails!" May Anna took her bare hands out of her pockets and joined the tall young mother, her little boy, and the leathery-faced woman all standing with hands extended for inspection.

"I 'customed to all kinds of house work," pleaded the grandmother.

"Over here, Ma'm, two for the price of one," bargained the young mother, her voice whining with desperation. "My little boy totes and carries while I work hard for you."

"How much do you want?"

"Seventy-five cent an hour?" the grandmother suggested as she wiped her watery eyes.

"Fifty cent for the two of us," auctioned the young mother, pushing her boy in front of the blonde. The white woman stepped back involuntarily as the boy came closer to her.

"What about you, do you wash and iron?" the woman inside the fur coat asked May Anna, noticing her silence.

"Sure do, ma'm," May Anna assured her. Now the grandmother was clawing at the woman's fur coat, pleading, "Forty-five cent an hour. I work hard for you."

A sudden gust of cold wind blasted through them and the woman retreated further inside her fur coat while peering at May Anna saying, "I need a plain cook. Can you do that?"

"Yes ma'm."

Suddenly the little boy became agitated and he tore off his overcoat and broke into a furious tap dance. He imprisoned the white lady with his antics, circling around her, arms pumping the air as his piercing soprano voice chanted in time to the staccato rhythm of his flying feet.

> My brown service
> Lasts long while
> Make you smile
> 'lasses sweet
> My brown skin service
> Shine yo feet

With one amused eye on the dancing boy and one ear on the haggling women, the fur coat continued to address May Anna.

"I'm expecting guests for lunch. Can you serve?"

"How much you paying?" May Anna asked the woman.

"How much you worth?" the fur coat inquired.

"Thirty-five cents an hour," interrupted the young mother whose son was now waving a shoeshine rag in the air as he continued to dance.

"With lunch and carfare for both of you?" came an incredulous muffled voice from inside the fur coat.

"Thirty cents an hour! Thirty cents!" shrieked leather-faced woman. "My Madam, I'm sound as a dollar. I'm fast and I don't eat much."

"Sold," said the fur-coated figure turning abruptly and walking toward her waiting Duesenberg. The bottom of her too long coat skimming the sidewalk as the old woman, bare head bowed down by the wind, shuffled behind her.

"Tomorrow is another day," May Anna thought as she recrossed Prospect Avenue and headed back into the icy winds. Ahead of her, a group of men passing a green bottle filled with red liquid among themselves huddled around a huge ash can in which a fire blazed. The flame light made their faces dance, shimmer, and glow in the cold air.

"G'day darlin," they said softly, tippin their hats and bowing as May Anna passed by.

She pulled her collar of her Navy peacoat around her ears, put her bare hands in her pockets, ignored the wind bellowing around her knees. Tommorrow will be better.

And now, May Anna stood before Mrs. Feral, trying to suppress her persistant cough and her anger.

"I don't think innocent children should suffer just because their mothers made a mistake," Mrs. Feral was saying.

"Virginia is not a mistake."

"If you don't have a husband then she is a mistake. That's the law."

Manman had been thirty-nine, she, twenty-two. "Girl," he had said, "I wish you would offer to let me do for you. I'm not ancient but I'm far from being a puppy. I won't marry you unless I own my own home so you won't have to worry. But until that time I'll work for you. Let me do for you." And they had lain naked, her body had glistened with his love.

Earlier, he had served her roast rabbit with a sassafras cream sauce, fried green onions, thinly sliced turnips flavored with salt pork and a special bottle of French Champagne saved from his war days. Another souvenir from those days was his gassed lungs and his limp, neither of which he ever mentioned. After dinner, while showing her his old certificate of stock in Garvey's Black Star Line, he gathered her in his arms saying, "It was a good dream. I'm not sorry I had it."

"I never heard anything about Garvey until I met you," May Anna said sorrowfully, thinking about Yula and tobacco and little pine carvings.

"Well you're hearing about him now," he said, biting her cheek. "I'll teach you everything." She left Hattie Jr.'s rear top floor two-room and moved downstairs in Manman's front apartment on the third floor. Even though books and old newspapers spilled out from every space and his African Legion uniform was displayed on the living-room wall like a painting, May Anna was happy.

One Sunday, Manman surprised her with a white taffeta puff-sleeved dress with a flared scalloped skirt and seed-pearl necklace. Then he reached up and removed his African Legion uniform from the wall. "It still fits," he said, relieved as he put it on the dark blue fitted jacked with gold buttons. A red braid encircled the armpit and shoulder on the left. A tan, narrow, leather belt ran diagonally from his left shoulder to the right one and met the tan belt at his waist.

"I'm a man of uniforms," he mused looking at his doorman's uniform of brown with large silver buttons. It also had gold braids but the braid ran down his right sleeve and was limp and fraying and unraveling. On the lapel was a tiny black, red, and green cross, so small it could pass unnoticed but big enough to remind him of his Garvey days. Also in that closet was his heavy wool army coat he wore in France, but he kept that hidden in the back.

"From U.S. Army to African Legion to Park Avenue doorman. A man of uniforms."

One Sunday, on a winter-tipped spring afternoon, Manman and May Anna walked to a low, flat, zinc-roofed building called Liberty Hall.

"I'd like to introduce you to my wife," he told several of his old UNIA friends. Cleota Johnson hugged her.

"He didn't try to impress you with his Knighthood in Garvey's Distinguished Order of Ethopia and all that old timey nonsense, did he?"

"I see you still got your cross," said Manman, eyeing the tiny cross on Cleota's lapel.

"Sure, I was a Black Cross nurse and proud of it. The difference between you and me is the difference between a tiny cross and the entire regalia 'cause that was then and this is now. Tell him, May Anna. It is nineteen hundred and thirty three! But he's a good man the same. A good ol' Race Man. Now honey you be sure to stop by my establishment someday. It's the best of its kind in Harlem."

It was, too. She attended Madame Cleota Johnson's School of Charm, Deportment, and Business, where she was taught "grooming, posture, carriage, and typewriting." In the throes of the Depression, my mother May Anna considered herself lucky when Cleota found someone who wanted a nice colored girl who could cook, clean, and typewrite for $35.00 a month.

May Anna typed Manman's letters also.

"Here is a letter acknowledging my fatherhood and informing them I want my child to bear my name. You know what will happen otherwise. What folks will call our child. You know the child will build an idea of who it is by the sound of his name. I'll have it notarized so you can take this letter and safekeep it."

She remembered another letter they labored over.

To President Roosevelt, Governor Dewey, Mayor LaGuardia and all elected representatives of the American Government:

I am a third generation American man. My grandparents went to their graves with the American government indebted to them for the labor stolen from them while they were in forced servitude.

But to bring you up to date, I served in the 369th regiment that was attached to the French Army because the American one was opposed to having Negro troops under its command. One night when on double sentry duty I was assaulted by the Germans. I received a serious wound in my left leg and gas in my right lung but continued to resist the enemy, fulfilling my responsibility of defending a long sector of front line trenches.

So you can see that although the American government has designated me a second class citizen I am a first class man. All these years, I have never been able to get my Disability. When the Veterans Bureau doctors examine me all they do is test my blood for V.D. This struggle for what is due me has been a long one and at this point I would now even take unjust compensation for my injuries.

*Kindly favor me with a righteous reply. In Truth and Justice, I
remain,*

> *Private James Manman Jackson*
> *Three Hundred and Sixty-Ninth U.S. Infantry, Regiment*
> *(former fifteenth New York National Guard)*

"A small house in Brooklyn," he told my mother when he finished reading. "Then we can get married but not before I can give you a house of our own." When she tried to tell him it didn't matter, he looked at her and said, "Of course it does. I'm a man."

A month before the Harlem Riots in 1935, May Anna opened the door and Manman rushed past her straight to the toilet. She could hear him gagging, retching, and moaning. Finally she pushed opened the bathroom door.

"I'm throwing them all up," sputtered my father, pushing her away.

"What?"

"White folks," sputtered Manman.

"White folks?" echoed May Anna uncomprehendingly. It was only after a long spell of gagging, spitting, and retching that he could reply.

"I been down the Veterans' Administration all day. Just thinking about them makes me want to spit up. Just thinking about them makes me feel like I swallowed rancid shit!"

"What happened?" my mother asked slowly beginning to understand.

"Nothing, that's just it. They grin and pretend they're trying to help me get my money. White folks will bless you to curse you and know they doin every kind of backhand dirt they can think of to keep me from getting what is rightfully mine. Why don't they come out and say it? 'We don't ever intend to compensate you for one old nigger lung and an old black leg.' I'd prefer that, then we can fight fist to face."

It was the winter of 1935 when almost every man he knew in Harlem was unemployed. But still he was shocked when he had to turn in his brown uniform with gold braids that he had worn for the past seven years.

"Cutbacks," said his boss softly, almost tenderly. "Tough times for everyone."

The next morning, en route to the employment office, from force of habit, Manman passed by the Park Avenue Arms, a wide building on the corner of Park Avenue and 37th Street whose white-washed stones gave off diamonds of light, even though it was ten blocks out of his way. Without his uniform, men and women for whom he had held the door open and hailed taxis every day for seven years did not recognize him The pale winter sun lit up the brass-framed entrance door, shooting off sparks of glinting brassy sunlight. Standing in front of his building in his same spot where he had stood; opening and closing the huge elaborate door; briskly smiling and bowing in one fluid movement as Manman had taught him; raising one arm for a cab and blowing a whistle with the other as Manman had shown him how to do was an energetic flaxen-haired adolescent he recognized as the desk clerk's son, with a ready smile on his cherubic face. He was even wearing his fucking uniform and had not bothered to repair the unraveling frayed braids. Manman stood across the street gazing at his old uniform in the pale sunlight.

"It was the light that was unbearable May Anna, the light. It was the morning light dancing on the frayed gold braids of my uniform making the shoulders of the white boy sparkle. It was the cold bright sunlight against the white stone building glimmering in the breeze, making my uniform glow, sparking his straw hair and framing his head like a halo; it was the light in the voices emerging from the elegant building and greeting my uniform. It is that light that weighs heavy on my mind," my father said, "weighs heavy on my mind."

A week later, it was that same lightness in the polite and official tone of the letter he read a letter from the V.A. that blinded him.

Dear Mr. Jackson

The Veterans Administration has undergone several changes since World War I. During that war we were known as The Bureau of War Risk and in 1920 we became the Veterans Bureau and presently we are the Veterans Administration. At this time our present organization is unable to find any records of your alleged service in the U.S. Army in World War I. Furthermore, the time limit for claims of alleged injuries in World War I expired in 1929. Therefore, we must disallow your claim of alleged injuries incurred in said war.

Ret. Lt. Commander Gipper Gowan

The following morning, a figure with a slight limp emerged from a front apartment three flights up. It wore a curly black wig, descended the stairs in the black oxford shoes worn by women who stand all day. A loose black dress was covered by a gray cloth coat with black velvet collar and pockets. In the right pocket lay a Want Ad torn from the *Daily Mirror:*

Miss Dixie wants Southern Gals
Sleep-ins. Every other Thursday off.

Manman touched his carefully curled black wig covered by pillbox hat with fashionable veil of Swiss dots. He stepped out into the street in the beginnings of a riot. As he emerged from his tenement, he was jostled, almost knocked down by a fleeing young boy in a top hat, tuxedo jacket, and blood-spattered undershirt who ran past him clutching a turkey and pursued by police with helmets and swinging billy clubs. Like high notes in a minor key the sound of shattered glass tinkled in the air. Gingerly he stepped aside, suprised but not really. Everyone knew that Harlem was going to boil over, and besides he had seen it all before and he had to get downtown to the agency before all the domestic jobs for women were gone. At 125th Street, he carefully wove his way in between mauled mannequins, broken glass, and trampled clothing. The air filled with screaming fire trucks and laughing people. Although most of the stores were emptied and their windows smashed, he caught sight of his reflection in the window of I. J. Silver Fur Emporium.

"After all," he told his reflection, "it's only another uniform."

Then he spied it and it was almost as if in the recesses of his mind he had conjured it up. It was perfect. May Anna's fur coat draped over a naked, haughty, bald-headed, pink mannequin.

"May Anna will love it, sir," said the mannequin to the red-bone man dressed like a woman.

"Yes, it's just her size," concurred Manman.

"What about the color, sir?" said the haughty plastic model still refusing to look at him.

"It's just her shade of mink."

"And the length. . . . Is it long enough, Sir?"

"Don't make it too long. It mustn't touch the sidewalk. May Anna's particular."

"How will you pay for it? Cash sir? Check sir? Sir? Sir?"

"Manhood. Self esteem. My black leg. My black lung."

"So Sorry that's not legal tender, nigger," said the pink dummy.

The store window screamed, shivered, and sprayed into zillions of glass splinters. My father was surprised at the weight of the rock in his palms and at the sight of his blood seeping into May Anna's fur coat that now lay in his arms. Suddenly he was defending a long sector of World War I American front line trenches. He knew he was wounded but continued to resist the advancing enemy, throwing rocks at a helmeted policeman's bullets from a prone position.

She didn't cry when Hattie Jr. told her that a female impersonator got killed trying to steal a woman's fur coat on 125th Street and in his wallet was an African Legion membership card that said that his name was Manman Jackson.

"O," May Anna said. Her mouth formed a perfect circle.

At the morgue, a smirking attendant returned a blood-spattered and bullet-riddled pillbox hat with a dotted Swiss veil that she had worn only on dress occasions, a curly wig, and a housedress that she had never seen before. Sign on the dotted line for your husband's clothes, smirked the amused morgue attendant.

In Manman's death May Anna saw justifiable rage, love, and loyalty, and she would not cry.

The African Legion buried him in the full dress of a Distinguished Knight in the Order of Ethiopa, his unsheathed sword shining in his casket.

"He was a man," said the Grand High Potentate, "who could put on a dress to go do a woman's job. He knew that his outward circumstances was not a definition of his character. He was a man of life who never stopped fighting back."

And still she did not cry.

The funeral service, the marching band two-stepping mournfully on the way to the grave, the jubilant second line returning from the grave and the party afterward with the delicious food was the end of a perfect death.

No tears yet.

Now that she was alone with a baby near to this life, May Anna had some decisions to make. She could stay in New York alone with a baby or return South. She dug out her cardboard suitcase and took out the old chammy cloth that contained Yula's whittled pine letters L I V E, red and yellow and orange and blue springing from one intricately carved green stalk like leaves on a stem.

They had been females, dependent on each other, and by leaving, she had broken the network of women who knew that they were all each other had. When Yula died, her guilt increased tenfold. But still, even after Manman's death in 1935, May Anna realized she still felt the same way she had in 1930. In spite of humiliation, unemployment, poor housing, and police brutality, May Anna was convinced, like hundreds of thousands others pouring into New York, that whatever she found here had to be better than what she left behind.

She carefully rewrapped Yula's letters in the ochre chammy cloth and gingerly returned the flimsy suitcase to a spot behind Manman's old doorman uniform. She would stand her ground. She would not retreat. She would stay in Harlem.

May Anna worked as a steam presser in a long large cellar in the garment district. She stood on her feet all day, bathed in clouds of steam raised by her heavy iron on damp cloth. It was under a restaurant, and the stench of food and greasy cooking was always in that basement workroom. There was a single window, always closed, which faced a blank wall, grimy with cobwebs and no daylight except for the light that came in through the cellar door, which was kept open winter and summer. Stray cats and beggars dug into the piles of garbage that clogged the yard.

"An ole hound dog stands by the door," she told Hattie Jr. as she soaked her swollen feet in hot water and Epsom salt. "He looks us over each time we leave to go to the bathroom to make sure we don't have any merchandise hidden under our clothes."

"My madam has a friend looking for a girl," Hattie Jr. informed her.

"No thank you. It's too close. I can't stand the look."

"The look?"

"Sure, they all got it. The men got it right from the git-go. And it don't take long for the women and kids to learn it. The look specially for 'the girl.' It looks like a ole tomcat's eyes before he stretch out to maul a mouse."

"And you don't get that look at the factory?"

"Sure but it ain't close on top of me, like it is some cracker's house. And I got plenty of company in the factory."

Hattie Jr. sucked her teeth, rolled her eyes and laughed as she patted May Anna's feet dry with a warm towel.

"Girl, think about your baby."

"Don't worry. I'm young and strong. I'll be okay."

It was true that she was young, but poor nutrition, poor venti-
lation, and long hours took their toll on her as they did on several
others in the epidemic of the White Plague in Harlem during the
thirties.

And now it was 1938 and the noise in her throat could not be
called just a cough. It had become such a permanent part of her
she hardly noticed it anymore, but Dr. Gold, a clinic doctor who
treated each patient as if they were wealthy private ones, was concerned.

"I want immediate chest X-rays," he ordered. He questioned
her about her nutrition, her apartment, her baby, her life. His
gentle eyes read her mouth, the color and texture of her skin.

Seven days after the X-rays had been taken at the Free Clinic,
Dr. Gold made a house call to her apartment on 140th street. "It's
just as I suspected. Moderately advanced."

"The consumption?" repeated May Anna, dry-eyed.

"In the throat."

"My baby?"

"She's okay. But you must go away to a sanitorium."

"But . . ."

"I don't think you understand," Dr. Gold said, forcefully, giving each word space and weight. "With what you have you must
hospitalize yourself immediately. Or you'll be dead and so will
everyone else around you."

"Okay, okay. You know how folks act, once you say you got the
consumption. Does anyone have to know what's wrong with me?

"Not as long as you make arrangements right away."

And so May Anna made arrangements in Mrs. Feral's parlor
agreeing to paying the foster mother $15.00 monthly because in
Mrs. Feral's words, "That measly allowance Sheltering Arms pays
foster mothers won't suffice."

*Virginia will live. She will live. At least she will live. This foster
mother is one of the stiff West Indian heifers that think they better.
Looking down on me cause I'm from the South. Cause I got a kid and*

no husband. Cause I'm dark. But that's how these monkey climbers get money and buy houses. Taking in children from the city all the while looking down their noses at us who have the kids.

"Although they put Hughes on Virginia's birth certificate, her father wanted her to have his last name, Jackson. Here's the paper to prove it," she said, and abruptly handed Mrs. Feral an envelope.

"Certificate says her name is Hughes. Not Jackson. Virginia Hughes."

"The birth certificate people got it wrong. They give her my last name just the same. Even though I showed them the papers he signed."

"Cheups." Mommi sucked her teeth and rolled her eyes. "You Americans make me sick! I'm law abiding and don't believe in questioning the authorities."

When May Anna left me in Mrs. Feral's living room the thunder of the apartment door she slammed behind her broke the dam inside of her and the tears finally burst through.

5

"Kill em! Dirty, filthy lepers! Polluting the air of decent people! TB is God's just punishment for their sins!" The bus teetered and they barely escaped being overturned at a traffic light on the east side of 23rd Street. May Anna cowered between the bus seats. She heard the crowd, which had just emptied out from the Chateau Gardens Ballroom after dancing to Fletcher Henderson and his band, curse the riders of the special bus to the sanitorium. Death don't have no mercy in this land, wailed the old man beside her between his bloody coughs. The driver had tried to make the trip in the dark, but the quarantined bus was spotted and and barely escaped the crowd's rage.

At Seaview Sanitorium on Welfare Island she counted the waves in the water. At night when she could no longer see the waves she would watch the blinking lights of the city opposite her window. At four A.M. the Empire State building was dark with a single row of muted lights and a solitary electric eye, its great search beams sweeping the heavens. When she tired of standing she would sit and watch a small tank of fishes that belonged to the floor supervisor. There was an elegant and swift emerald and gold fish she called Sugar Ray Robinson. When she leaned down to get a closer look she could see him looking at her straight in the eye. Soon she asked the same question everyone else asked whenever the doctors examined her. Till you get well enough to go home, they always replied.

And so she began to draw. She started sketching images imbedded deep within her, rainbow baobab trees and crimson seascapes, fields of streaming sky shimmering in blues. Faces of flowers, limbs of humans and bodies of animals joined together in mythological forms, and always unchanged, impervious to the melange of riotous colors beneath it, a big fat golden sun. May Anna drew everything except the face of the little girl that was always looming before her. If I am to survive this disease I got to stay up. Doctor said the blues is bad for consumption, she thought, as she unsuccessfully attempted to stifle her cough.

The second year outside the sanitorium walls a war with Germany was about to explode. Inside the sanitorium walls the fight with death did not eliminate other wars. In the bed next to her, in halting English, barely able to breathe, a patient angrily objected to a darky's presence. She wondered if God was mad at her for something she did or did not do. She wondered if her family, her race had a curse on them as some people said. She wondered if her daughter would forget or forgive her. She wondered, when people die do they go up or down or just out?

In her third year at Seaview, after three months had passed, the doctor stopped by her bed and said, "You may go home any time you like now but remember, you have a cavity. Yes, a negative-open cavity, negative bacilli. It will take time to heal. But it will if you get plenty of physical and mental rest. You must have a room to yourself where you can go in and shut the door. You must live at home like you do here."

The day May Anna was released from the sanitorium she went straight to 120th Street. Mommi pushed me into the parlor where a strange woman sat waiting. She constantly pulled her left ear with her left hand and in her right hand she held some letters on a stem painted in different colors. The strange lady smiled at me and revealed a wide gap between her two front teeth. Her thick, soft, woolly hair was gathered in a fluffy ball on top of her head. She ran toward me arms outstretched. Her pleading crying eyes were hot needles on my skin.

"Ooo oo ooh," she chanted brokenly. She squeezed me tightly as I howled and kicked my legs furiously, straining toward Mommi. She released me so abruptly, I stumbled.

"Don't you know me? Don't you remember who I am?" I hid behind Mommi's warm bulk.

"I'm your ole lady," she pleaded with outstretched arms. Terrified, I screamed.

"You just stroll in here like it is the Dew Drop Inn and folks supposed to be glad to see you?" said Mommi to the lady who seemed to be angry.

"I got a right. She's mine. My kid," the lady said, grabbing me.

"Leave her alone," Mommi commanded as I shrank from the strange lady's touch.

But in a cracking half-voice she kept murmuring, "I'm your ole lady," over and over. She caught me and put her face close to mine. Her bitter smell of perfume and powder, pain and wine covered me and I wriggled away from her and ran. She never came to visit me again.

After that visit May Anna set out with a vengeance to make a home and reclaim me. But she had lost her old apartment and even Hattie Jr. was reluctant to live with her. It was the early forties and tuberculosis was still the plague of the century and anyone who had ever had it was always suspect. So she had to rent a room with a toilet in the hall but at least it was on the ground floor. It was two years before she mastered her stenography course, finally got fast enough so that she took a civil service examination. May Anna stayed away from 120th Street. She had no extra money to smooth her way with Mrs. Feral. And she could not stand to see her little girl frightened of her and hide behind that woman, couldn't stand Mrs. Feral's sweeping and disapproving gaze. You should thank your lucky stars, they told her at Sheltering

Arms. Lots of children like yours can't even get in a foster home. A colored social worker, tall with shiny long black hair, by the name of Mrs. LeNoire, got angry when she complained about Mrs. Feral. Two more years sped by, years in which May Anna passed four or five exams, each time way down on the list. Years spent waiting and hoping for an appointment and taking other exams. She had haunted the government agencies, seeking work. Even though it was now 1946 and Truman had ordered the Civil Service to desegregate, when she entered an office she saw the uncontrollable amusement, disdain, and hatred in the faces of those who conducted the charade of interviewing her.

She had a plan. The only way she could achieve any status was to become a respectable married woman. A woman living alone didn't stand much chance. With a man around there was a big difference in everyone's attitude. Besides, when there were two working, if one got sick the other one could carry on and there would still be food and the rent would be paid and the sooner she could set up housekeeping and reclaim me. But as she went from man to man, each affair leaving a bitter aftertaste, a truth rose up in her like bile, one she had been pushing back since childhood. There was a war between black men and women. Not the subtle, unspoken, natural tensions in the ongoing battle of the sexes but a full-out genocidal conflagration between the brothuhs and sistuhs. She had grown up in a family, no, a community of women, with barely a visible man. The only evidence of a male presence somewhere at one time or another was that there was never any lack of pregnant women among them. But now that she was a woman grown she realized that with each generation, the strife between the black man and black woman was no family secret. Nowhere but in Harlem did she see men beating women openly on the streets without being disturbed. Crowds would gather to watch but no one wanted to interfere in what they called private business. After they had been entertained enough the cops would break it up. Maybe.

And the preferences of black men were legendary. There was a classic Harlem joke circulated that went like this: A black man placed the following advertisement in the paper:

WOMAN WANTED

RACE UNIMPORTANT

IF YOU WHITE YOU IN

BUT IF YOU BLACK

MUST HAVE JOB,

STRAIT HAIR

VERY BRITE SKIN!

Besides, she never seemed to prosper when there was a man in her life. They could always find her money even if it was only a dollar bill, no matter where she put it, they could get it even if it was in the bank. They were always drunk, broke, and evil and trying to soothe them was beyond her dark-skin powers. Even way back then it was a jungle in Harlem and black women were the prey. Of course she could have been nice to some white gentleman. Seemed like every time she turned around someone was always whispering to her about some white gentleman. As things went from bad to worse she gave it plenty of thought. She saw the moist warm looks of white men on the subways brazenly appraising her breasts and behind, trying to lock her eyes as they peeped over their newspapers and spread open their thighs. It was bad enough she had to put up with white folks all day to earn a living. She certainly didn't want to have to deal with them in her bed.

In 1948, Nat King Cole's "Straighten Up and Fly Right" was out on 45 r.p.m. and on 148th Street and St. Nicholas Avenue in a rear kitchenette May Anna was thirty-six years old while on 120th Street I had just turned a sullen twelve. We were separated by a few city miles and ten and a half years. I am sure both of us passed each other in the Harlem streets without recognition. A common-law husband wanted to kill her when he found out she had been to the sanitorium for the cure. Instead, he broke her nose, took her purse, and moved out. A woman has to survive. A woman has to live. That was the one prayer she had for her child. Live. Live. Live. Even in the throes of tuberculosis when every breath was painful, each one was a silent prayer of "live." With every cell of her faith she believed that somehow I received her one-word message. "Live." What was left without the breath of life? For she knew as long as a woman survived she had a chance. This belief in life had enabled her to come up North and leave her own mother in search of her own life. It had given her the strength to leave me with Mommi, although she could never bring herself to officially sign adoption papers.

Paradoxically, May Anna hoped the very traits that made her and Mommi butt heads, Mommi's strong will, aura of moral superiority, and enterprising nature, might rub off on me. Of course, not full blown like Mrs. Feral. Just a little bit might be just what I needed in order to get further in life than she had. After the sickness, after the men, her relentless economic struggle, she told herself that I was better off without her. Peace of mind was what she wanted now. She tried various churches, but only when she reached Heaven did she find God. She found him when her old friend Hattie Jr. took her for a sumptuous Sunday meal for fifteen cents at the Father Divine Peace Mission on 129th Street and Lenox Avenue.

In the center of the banquet table in Heaven, in a natty cream-colored suit, silk shirt, and gleaming Florsheim shoes, God sat, blessing each dish that Happy Sweet, sitting on his right hand, passed to Him. He blessed every platter in each course of the huge feast. One by one as the angel passed Him heaping platters, He-Who-Is-The-One inserted a serving spoon or fork and intoned:

Every Morsel
Every Sip

Health to body
Peace to mind
Peace everybody,
Peace be thine.

With a flourish The-Bringer-Of-All-Blessings dispersed one dish to the left and another to the right, sending them down the long tables on both sides. White crepe paper twirled gently from wall to wall in the ceiling above and curled around a huge gold chandelier that spread a soft white light. Tall cones of white linen napkins rooted in sparkling glasses stood like sentinels before each gleaming white plate. Only soft candlelight from small candle holders softened the glare of the relentless white banquet table.

After her first visit, May Anna renounced all wordly thoughts and became an Angel in Heaven and on Sundays stood at the right hand of Father during his famous Sunday feasts. The Angel passed platters of steaming fluffy rice, leafy Swiss chard and hominy, mushrooms, candied yams, and creamed corn to Father, who held his hand over each plate for a blessing. She passed platters of plump sausages that reminded her of infant thighs, slices of smoked Virginia ham, halves of young and tender chicken, succulent roasts of lamb, juicy, thick pork chops, passed from her hand to God's touch for his blessing. When she gazed at the glistening meats on silver platters the intoxicating aromas sent strong, sharp, healthy hunger pains into the Angel's stomach. May Anna loved feeling hungry instead of nauseated by the smell of food. God taught his followers that good health equaled a good appetite. Every Sunday he weighed his entire Heaven and reprimanded those Angels who had lost weight. When his new Angel saw the laden baskets, her face radiated with the same beatific smile which had inspired The-Understander to bless her with her Angelic Name, Happy Sweet. Happy Sweet beamed to Father as she began passing bread trays. He was her perfect husband. Now, the egg-yellow cornbread squares. God provided. Cracked wheat. God comforted. Whole wheat. Rye. Crackers. Sugared doughnuts. God Blessed. The final course consisted of great bowls of gelatins in neon lemon, lime, and tangerine. Happy Sweet was standing in the Rapture. Platters of huge slices of coconut and chocolate cake. Thank you Father. Tub-like bowls of home-made ice cream. Peace was Truly Wonderful. And every Sunday, Heaven was filled with an earth-shaking, booming baritone as God sang to his congregation:

> Well I don't want no sorrow in my heart
> Don't want sorrow in my heart
> For if you are sorrowful,
> So am I
> But if you rejoice
> I rejoice with you.

The masses in Harlem may have been unemployed, hungry, and downpressed, but inside Heaven they were uplifted, well fed, and full of peace.

But in Father's Heaven disease was just an outward sign of inner sinfulness, and sickness among his Angels was not tolerated by God. Death is the last sin to be overcome, taught Father, the last evil to conquer. You can do it only if you have enough faith. In the late forties a diagnosis of laryngeal turberculosis was a death sentence within a death sentence.

Expelled from Heaven because of a relapse and back in the sanitorium overlooking the East River, May Anna was determined to conquer. She focused on the laryngeal mirror and the healing ritual that she had to perform every day. On her last day, May Anna gazed at the laryngeal mirror custom made for patients with laryngeal turberculosis. She twisted the large mirror attached to the head of her bed, carefully attempting to reflect the sun's rays, reflect and beam them down to a smaller, throat-sized mirror with aluminum coating that she could insert in her larynx in order to radiate the lesions in her throat. Whenever she did this she could get a good view of the interior of her diseased and wasted larynx. Ten minutes was the maximum an ulcerated larynx could tolerate concentrated solar radiation, but the nurse was not on the alert. May Anna clasped the tube-like instrument tightly, twisting its reflecting mirror rapidly toward the sun. Determined to live, she held the laryngoscope, bent on getting more of the sunlight's healing radiation, sucking up the sun's reflections until, too hot to hold, she dropped the mirror, but not before it set her throat on fire.

There was no one to notify. She had lost contact with Hattie Jr., Sheltering Arms, or any of her old life. And on 120th Street I was still hoping and waiting.

6

I grew tired of waiting in that courtroom. The gray-veined white marble, the gleaming wood, the empty air, its flat silence, the men in front of me, a granite-faced judge with his clerks huddled around him who were passing papers and whispering in each other's faces were woven into a scenario that I seemed to be watching from far away. I knew my future would be, in a large part, remembering this day. In an effort to escape the present I mused had my own mother ever thought about what kind of people she had left me with?

They were all transplanted Bermudians who came to New York in 1927. On their second day in America, Percival and Winnie Feral and her older sister, Sylvia, emerged out of the darkness of 145th Street and Lenox Avenue subway station and went straight to the Bermuda Benevolent Association. There they were given the name of a real estate agency that specialized in "coloured" tenants and the addresses of some factories that were looking for girls to do piecework. The job they found paid ten cents for flat pieces, a nickel more for the complicated garments. That meant they really had to be fast in order to make enough to come back the next day. Sylvia, a talented dressmaker, caught on right away, but it was Winnie who was all thumbs and who found out that the factory owner had his own system of breaking in green, clumsy operators.

In a back room where he had called Winnie he said, you look like a girl who is worried about something. Don't be. I'll keep you. I know you'll catch on, won't you? All my girls do. It was a storeroom with walls of cloth making the air dry and lint filled. An old man smelling of garlic with hair sticking out of his ears, he put his lips against the back of Winnie's neck, his arm around her waist and said, I never get in trouble over one of my gals. I just let her go if she wants. His rheumy eyes stared at her as if she were a bug under his microscope as he began to rub himself. You think I'm going to bother you but I don't go any further than this. When she walked past him to return to her machine his arthritic fingers pinched, patted, and rubbed her behind.

What did he say? whispered Sylvia as she sat back down.

Nothing, he just told me to take it easy and I would catch on, Winnie lied, ignoring the knowing looks of the other operators. After all, it was nothing to get upset about. Better her than Sylvia. She still had the job. He had hardly touched her. She would take ten baths when she got home. There was rent to be paid, food to be bought; she could not afford to give in to any weak feelings. Soon, she was the operator finished with her part of the garment first, and very soon the fast tempo of the machine was much easier and seemed as natural to her as when she sewed at home.

Mr. Feral got a job as a stoker in a General Motors Plant in Kearny, New Jersey, which he was to keep for thirty years. He worked all the time but made little money, his wages a weak but steady trickle. As long as he could practice on his cornet and study his Bible, Mr. Feral did not give much thought to anything on an earthly level. He was a steady, hard-working man satisfied with any odd piece of a job. When Rose was born, and Mrs. Feral could no longer go downtown to the garment district with Sylvia, their household was in trouble.

Luckily, with the groundswell of southern migrants to New York, the need for foster homes grew urgent. But did she really want to take care of somebody else's children? Who knew what kind of garbage blood ran in their veins? They were the illigitimate children of those other black folks who were loose and lazy, had no sense of family, no sense of decency. But she did like babies and they did need the money and anyhow it would only be for a short time till times got better, so why not?

Mrs. Feral became known at Sheltering Arms Children's Service as an excellent nurturer, and many children were placed under her care. They were all infants whose mothers reclaimed them, usually before a year. She had a green thumb with babies and very small children, and like the tekenbakias, snake plants, and morning glories in her living room, her infants thrived.

She understood the secret of herbs and roots, the tides and seasons of the moon, was known to make short hair long and wasn't I living proof that she could make an inherited weak chest strong by good food, regular doses of cod liver oil, hot mustard poultices, and a handmade satin bag tied around my neck that contained asafetida leaves, garlic, and camphor balls to repel germs and other evils?

But even as a child still small enough to climb up into the warm valley of Mommi's lap or grab her hand as I walked or to cry when she was out of my sight I smelled the tension in the apartment.

When the wars broke out between us, I used to wonder between beatings about her past. What was she like as a girl? Did she ever think of her husband as someone she could love and respect? Had Mr. Feral always been a "jackleg preacher" as Mommi called him, traveling from place to place living off of donations until they married? Why did they emigrate from Bermuda to New York City? What did she leave behind in Bermuda? What conditions did she have to tolerate and what was the price of her forbearance? Why did she dominate the household with an unrelenting psychic terrorism that rendered her husband and older sister fearful and spineless?

Kelvin began to move and fret in my arms and I was brought back to the courtroom that somehow had emptied during my reverie. The judge and his clerks were conferring in his chambers, Mrs. Wallings leaned over and whispered. I felt as if I had been granted a small reprieve and returned to my past.

I am in the kitchen sitting in my high chair. In the room is my family, Mommi, Daddy, Aunt Syl, and Rose. On the stove is a dancing teapot with a thread of steam beckoning to me. I lean over to try to hold the curling smoke in my fingers and tip over my high chair catapulting downward. Suspended, the the second before I hit the floor, hands catch me, raise me up, brown arms encircle me and in that moment I know that these are the gods of my being and no outside harm, not even gravity, can penetrate their fortress of brown arms.

7

We lived on 120th Street and Lenox Avenue, a quiet street with rows of narrow brownstones on both sides of the long block owned mainly by Jamaicans and Barbadians and Grenadians. The limestone building where we lived was the only apartment in the block. In it, Mr. and Mrs. Feral and her family were surrounded mostly by newly arrived Virginians and North Carolinians. While Lenox Avenue was an unknown territory peopled with unsavory strangers, our street was a haven of security, a self-contained community where folks knew the comings and goings of one another and generally treated each other with good will and politeness.

Next door to us was Mount Olivet Baptist Church, formerly Temple Israel. It was a grand limestone temple with four separate columns of steps leading up to four pillars constructed in a Roman Classical style. On hot summer days like this one the rehearsing choir's voices spilled out into the street, a faint rim on all other sounds.

> Let us break bread together
> On our knees
> Yes, on our knees.

"Amsterdam News! Read All About It! Lynch Bill Fai . . . Harlem Numbers

"King Jai . . . Wife catches Hu . . . NAACP Sues . . . Amsterdam! Get Your Damn News Here!" bellowed the rotund, gray-haired news man running up one side of the street and down the other wearing his apron stuffed with the Harlem weekly. On his heels came Scissors-Man with his wagon filling the air with the metallic hiss of knives and scissors being sharpened.

"WoooTeeeeeMelllllon!" warbled a Georgia truck-farmer as his horse clip clopped up and down the street dropping balls of manure along the way. "WoooTeeeeMeeLllllooon!" the farmer repeated. "Sweet red meat ah loves to eat, suck the seeds 'tween mah teeth. Woooomeellooon," he crooned in a high soprano up and down the scale.

"Deux! Trois and a Four!" roared General Parlez-Vous, marching in time with his inner drum and fife wearing his World War I helmet and boots, carrying a rifle in one hand and saluting the world with the other. Mr. Bennett, the super, who was standing on the stoop, murmured "Crazy ol' sucker" into the whiskey bottle he lifted to his head and drained.

Down the street came Tiny Tim, the ice cream man, a sparkling navy blue-black man dressed in brilliant white from his cap to his shoes and speedily pushing an equally white cart with a row of silver bells on the handle bars.

As he jangled the bells he sang out his wares above his own din, "Popsicles! Icesicles! Fudgesicles! No Creamsicles!"

When Mrs. Feral needed ice for the icebox, I flew out of our apartment and bounded down the stairs two at a time, flying down toward the corner of Lenox Avenue toward Dom's wagon permanently stationed on the corner. I whizzed by Miss June and Miss Sharon, sitting quietly breast-feeding their babies on the steps of the brownstones where they rented furnished rooms with cooking privileges, no linens supplied.

"My mother said send her twenty-five cents worth," I told Dom the ice man, handing him the quarter. On the side of the wagon were little brown paper bag flags, impaled on a stick and scrawled in red crayon, "Ice, 5 sent, 10 sent and 15 sents." Dom was thickset, short, Italian and ruddy with slick, black hair. I studied him, remembering Godfather Wilfred, the old Garveyite's voice shouting, "The Italians got dark complexions because Hannibal the Moor crossed those Alps and kicked Italy's ass and now all they are now are just some more white folks pretending not to be black!" as he brought down his gnarled, ashy fist on our kitchen table.

"Do you know Hannibal?" I asked the ice man as he grabbed an ice pick and chiseled a huge rectangle from the ice block in his wooden wagon. He smiled at me, not understanding a word of English, as he strapped a thick burlap-covered pad on his right shoulder. Grabbing the frozen rectangle with a pair of black iron tongs, the ice man squatted down and hoisted the ice block up on his shoulder with one quick movement. I followed him as he trudged down the block, up two flights of stairs and down our long hall to our kitchen where in our icebox he deposited the block of ice, already melting.

My errand done, I returned to look through the metal bars of the window guards at the street below. Gazing up and down the street I braided a white satiny paper ribbon into my hair. As the hot afternoon sun went in, Renee and Rosalie, Fat Helen, and Lil Armstrong tumbled out in the street loaded down with jumprope, balls, and boxes of colored chalk.

"Come downstairs and play with us," taunted Helen, knowing I wasn't allowed. "If you come down we'll have enough to jump 'Chase The' in hot pepper time."

I wiped my tears with the back of my hand as Daddy, looking at me, suddenly turned to Mommi and said, "Winnie, let the girl go outside for a while."

"No," replied Mommi. "Look at her body. It's too mature for children's games."

"For God's sake, she's eight years old." And then turning to me, "Go on outside for a while," Daddy said. "And stay right in front of the house," he yelled as I ran downtairs quickly escaping.

In the street, weaving between the traffic, Yellow Eric was streaking around the bases laughing all the way. On the sidewalk, Rosemarie, Janie, Teena, and Thelma, from 119th Street, had joined us so that there was a long line of girls waiting to jump Double-Dutch.

"You can turn," said Fat Helen, handing me her mother's clothesline that served as the jump rope. I put it around my waist and began turning, chanting and singing with the rest of the girls as the jumpers executed our orders.

> *gonna touch ground and turn around*
> *gonna hop and skip and take a dip*

I was happy. My blood-clotted fingernails eagerly turned the jumprope. I was just anxious for my turn to jump rope. I just wanted to get a chance before I had to go back upstairs. Finally I was next.

> *gonna somersault*
> *and jump double time*
> *hands on the hip and the old knee bend*
> *do the right hand stand, wave left leg in the air*
> *if you do you a friend of mine*

I twisted and turned my body following the crowd's commands. I could do anything they called out. From my windowsill I had studied their best moves and created some of my own. No longer made of bone and flesh I jumped high, I bent low, I somersaulted in midair and touched the ground leaning backward gleefully drinking in the crowd's admiration.

> *Scissor legs*
> *Go go go!*

Suddenly, the rope jerked, I tripped over it and fell to my knees. "You out, you out, you . . . are . . . out!" exulted Fat Helen who was one of the turners.

"I'm not. You jerked it. I felt it." I paid no attention to my scraped knee and looked up at Helen. Her eyes were full of malice and mockery as she looked at me and then at the crowd who circled around us, smelling blood.

Helen was the ringleader of the block and I wanted to be in her clique but she would have nothing to do with me in public. I scrambled to my feet and faced her.

"Cry baby. Go and tell your stuck up ma."

"I get to finish my jump because you pulled it." She was only a year older than I but already had breasts. Even the boys didn't mess with Helen. No one dared tease her about her size.

"Mahhhngo squeezing coco haid," she said in a fake West Indian accent. "Gimme some bahnanas." Everyone dutifully screamed with laughter.

"I am not."

"Are so."

"Liar."

"If you ain't a monkey-chaser why you wearing those monkey bracelets, banana head?"

"Cotton picker."

"Let's see that smelly bag you wear under your clothes. I know you got one. All monkey chasers wear one."

"I do not," I said, involuntarily touching the asafetida bag Mommi had put around my neck to ward off germs. "You stinkin chitlin eater!"

"Oh yeah? I hear you yelling and screaming . . . Ooooo Ahhhhhh oooo! when you are getting your licks," she hollered in a grotesque imitation of me much to the crowd's delight.

"I do not," I lied.

"Monkey chaser live in a tree," Helen chanted. "Monkey chaser pee the bed. Monkey chaser wear bright red."

"You big dummy. Everybody knows you can't even read because you're from down home," I retorted.

"O yeah?"

"Yeah."

"So what? Least I got a mama."

"So do I."

"No you don't. Your real ma throwed you away. I heard her tell you that one night when you was getting a whipping. Ahhh-hooooooaaa," she mocked me again.

Pointing my forefinger at her I gave her the curse saying, "Everything you say about me goes back to you and your whole generation. Ten times!"

"Don't point at me. My mother's not dead," screamed Helen hysterically.

"OoooooooooooOoo!" chanted the circle of girls, anxious for blood. "She sounded on you. She's talking about your Moother!"

Then they shoved me on top of Helen, and scratching, punching, crying, and clutching each other we both fell to the sidewalk.

"Mrs. Feral may not be your mother but you stuck up, seditty, and smell of fishcakes just like her."

Every punch I could deliver to Fat Helen was for Mommi. I spread open my hands as I had often seen Mommi do and then at the right second when she was off guard, my spread-open hands flew to Helen's face with a resounding backhand slap.

Helen went straight for my hair and ripped my ribbon out of my hair along with a fistful of my hair.

"Give 'em room," the crowd chanted, widening the circle to give us more room to roll around on the sidewalk.

> *Let us praise God together*
> *On our knees*
> *Yes on our knees.*

Rehearsing choir voices from Mount Olivet Baptist Church floated above the taunts of the delighted mob.

Something primal burned within me. "No one," I thought," has the right to talk about my mother, even if she is Mrs. Feral."

When I fall on my knees
With my face to the rising Sun
O! Lord Have mercy
If you please.

A piercing scream from Helen jolted me to my senses. My eyes focused on Helen backing away from me, holding her bleeding lower lip. My teeth marks were on the fleshy part and there were pinpoints of blood around the punctured flesh. I wasn't sorry. I only wished that I had succeeded in ripping her lip from her face so she would be unable to say anything about Mommi again.

Still howling with pain, Helen continued backing away from me lisping through her swollen lips, "I'm gonna kickth yourth ass."

"COME UP STAIRS THIS MINUTE," blasted Mommi's voice, scattering everyone like refuse in a sudden gust of wind. I stood in the empty, quiet street. My shiny white candy-paper ribbon floated in a stream of sewer water. It swirled around in circles, pushed and pulled by gusts of summer breezes.

Back upstairs, kneeling on the floor, locked in a vise of her thighs, my hands resting on her plump knees, I bent over as Mommi parted my hair with her fingers and examined the bloody bruises on my scalp.

"Ooooow," I protested as she painted my bruises with iodine.

"Serve you right for fighting in the street like a common thug." Then, dipping her finger tips into a concoction of aloe and castor oil she parted my hair, rubbing in the mixture slowly and saturating my entire scalp.

"Who is my mother?" I asked as I leaned back against the pillow of her stomach that made a soft bulge in her cotton house dress. "And where is she?" I persisted.

Thwaaack! went her comb on my head.

"I told you to bend over!" she said exasperated. "May Anna came to see you once when you were four years old. That was almost five years ago."

"Then why don't you adopt me?" I asked as she ran her fingers through my hair to make sure all the kinks were untangled.

"Because you are a thankless child, stubborn and ungrateful with a mind of your own." Mommi said holding my face in her hands and twisting my head to see if she had parted my hair straight.

"I want my name to be like yours," I pleaded.

"Your name is Hughes just like your mother," she said pulling extra hard on a tangle, "but if you behave and promise not to get any more whippings maybe . . ."

"I will. I'll be good."

"But what if May Anna should pop up?" asked Mommi, gazing at my head, satisfied with her handiwork.

"Let her, I won't go with her if she does," I answered.

"Just when you're old enough to work and pay me back for all I've done for you that's when she'll show up again and take you."

"Mommi, I hate May Anna. I won't go with her."

"I've seen it happen before. I'm just fattening frogs for snakes."

"Am I West Indian like you?"

"No. Your mother was from the South."

"Oh, " I said, disappointed.

"And I'm no West Indian."

"But Helen said . . ."

"The next time she calls you a West Indian, tell her Berumuda is not in the Carribean, it is in the Atlantic Ocean and we are British subjects, not West Indians."

"Will I always be just a foster child?"

"No one has to know our business."

"Everyone knows cause you told Mrs. Field and she told Helen. That's what we were fighting about."

"It's nothing to fight about," Mommi comforted me. "You can't help it. And if you just do as I tell you maybe you can overcome your background." Suddenly standing she continued,

"Meantime I'm going downstairs and give that back-country Eva Field a piece of my mind for putting my business in the street."

From that day on, though publicly civil to one another, a silent war raged between the two women behind closed doors. "That cotton picking witch is cooking up one of her tricks," Mommi would announce as she sniffed the air angrily whenever the smell of camphor and burning sage wafted from Mrs. Field's apartment. Or whenever the radiators and pipes began mysteriously hissing and clanking at odd hours for no apparent reason, Mommi would throw salt in all directions "to protect us from downstairs." Periodically, all our floors would be sprinkled with a special holy water solution that would repel any evil that might be seeping through our walls from downstairs. In our hallway there was a spot that was supposed to correspond to Mrs. Field's bedroom one flight down. In that spot, incense and candles were perpetually lit. The neighbors kept track of the battle, eagerly listening to as much as each woman revealed.

Their choice for the winner was purely a matter of ethnic loyalty. The West Indians thought obeah unbeatable, while the Southerners believed their Hoodoo to be more effective in the modern world. Meanwhile, away from our apartments, although it was taboo, Fat Helen and I played and fought with each other whenever we could.

8

Excursions outside of Harlem were events to prepare for. Even the weekly shopping trip on the east side in the eighties to Germantown where Mommi and I shopped and returned by bus with overflowing brown paper bags with raffia handles was a special occasion.

"I shop all over, breaking my back, hauling shopping bags all over New York just to buy good food. I should just settle and feed everyone in this house the garbage they sell in Harlem," she would intone every Saturday while making sure my hair was braided and my legs vaselined. That task completed, she turned me around and stared at me, demanding I looked her in the eye as she gave me her instructions for traveling downtown.

"Do not let any white folks rub your head. Your head is not a rabbit's foot. Hold it high. When they ask you to dance for them, refuse and never take any money white folks offer you. In fact no money from strangers, period. Understand?" Then donning her navy blue shopping dress and carrying a black patent leather pocketbook in one hand and grabbing my hand in the other she walked down the street like an empress moving among serfs, head high, eyes straight ahead, but aware of everyone and everything.

Standing at the bus stop, I hope for a seat by the window. Kneeling in my seat, pressing my nose against the window, I drink in the passing scene. The bus gently rolls past a huge vacant lot where a forest of weeds as tall as trees sway gently in an autumn breeze. Soon, we pass by P.S. 184 and I wonder what Miss Matlin is doing at this very moment. Now we are in front of the Regent Theater, an old dilapidated and cavernous movie house unused for years. Fire escapes zigzag along the side of the building, which was once a famous place in Harlem's "heyday." I wonder about this "heyday" that grownups always speak about and find it difficult to visualize a time when whites came uptown to mingle. The smooth amble of the bus becomes a jerky, monoxide, belching lurch as throngs of shoppers and vendors begin to overflow from the sidewalks into the street. As the bus fitfully starts and stops, dark complexions permutate into varying browns as people get off and on the bus and loud bursts of Spanish begin to pepper the air.

"Bese me Bese me muchoooooo," croons a man in the back of the bus.

"Bese me cula. Shut up," answers a black man in the front.

We were now on Park Avenue and 116th Street where underneath the elevated trains is the City Market. I think how the roaring of the trains overhead, mixed with the unfamiliar chatter of Spanish, the pungent throngs of Jamaicans, Barbadians, and Puerto Ricans, all who come to buy manioc, breadfruit, saltfish, male pawpaw root, sour tamarind, sweet broom, minny root, Bengue balm, and countless other hard-to-get island fruits, vegetables, herbs, and spices and the hodgepodge of glaring colors combined with the onslaught of odors from the market stalls always makes me dizzy, irritable, and slightly nauseous. I'm glad I'm inside the bus and that we won't be shopping here today. As the bus turns on Lexington Avenue the street vendors and their sprawling wares suddenly disappear. At 95th Street, almost as if someone pressed a magic button, the crumbling buildings with huge boarded-up cavities vanish and in their places wide ornate apartment buildings with elegant doormen materialize; the chaos of the streets is overtaken by stillness; the melange of fuschias, chartreuses, and scarlets has thinned into quiet pastels; no longer is there every gradation of black, brown, and yellow in the passing faces; we are trapped in a world of white people.

At 86th Street the bus stops right in front of "Werner's Prime Cuts." When Mommi and I push open the door and enter the long narrow shop filled with customers, the murmur of "Schwartze" is audible and amused glances run through the current of customers, standing in a long line, grasping small cardboard squares with black crayon numbers scrawled on them, waiting to be called.

"Fifty-seven," calls out Mr. Werner, the butcher.

"Here," says Mommi fishing a cardboard number from a collection in her purse. "I'm next." She never got her number from the wire basket by the store's entrance. She either pulled out a number from her shiny patent-leather pocketbook or found one in the soggy sawdust of the butcher shop floor. There are scowls and even disputes but she always wins.

"Just a little game between me and the white folks," she always whispers to me. "They don't have to be first all the time."

No matter how crowded the butcher shop is, we never have to wait too long before our number is called. An old man with weak blue eyes looks at me and smiles. He reaches for my head and I duck just in time. The butcher, Mr. Werner, has pink skin, blue eyes, and white hair and is the closest resemblance to a live Santa Claus I have ever seen. His blood-spattered apron covers a mound of a stomach and in an unctuously hearty manner he proudly exhibits choice cuts of meat.

"I got chicken feet for you for this week. Yah?"

"The feet make the best soup."

"What time is soup. I come to your house for some. Yah?"

A pleasant-faced woman with a little girl watches me as I straddle a high two-legged wooden stool and with my feet draw stick figures on the floor in the damp sawdust. Smiling at me she opens her purse and pulls out two pennies saying, "I bet you can dance."

From the butcher shop we go to the Atlantic & Pacific Supermarket on the corner. Marching up and down the aisle, talking to the shelves, Mommi chooses canned goods she will store in the kitchen closet in case there is another Depression. I stick out my tongue at a boy who makes cross-eyes at me and Mommi almost catches me. At the checkout counter we stand on an endless line. Once again the weekly shopping ritual has been completed, and loaded down with overflowing brown paper shopping bags, we board the bus again and head back uptown.

However, in the rare trip beyond the city, we all happily lugged a wicker basket of fried chicken, an iron pot of peas and rice, and two jugs of lemonade on the bus and train to the ferry that would take us thirty-five miles up the Hudson to Bear Mountain State Park. Mommi and Aunt Syl had gotten the idea while they were trying to catch a breeze standing on the fire escape gazing down at the steaming pavement.

"I can't get a good pawpaw in New York and I need it for my indigestion."

"What about the City Market on Park?"

"I did and they don't. At least no pawpaw like home."

"You gotta ask for papaya. That's what they call it here."

"Remember how it used to smell back home this time of year . . ."

"Lilies and juniper wood."

"I can feel how the lilies padded the ground."

"I can smell how they perfume up the air."

"Member how we used to make baskets out of palmetto?"

"O for some cassava pie right now."

"Or a cooling drink of sorrel."

"Let's go on a picnic. Let's get out of the city."

We were going on a boat on a river to the country! "The country" was any place with trees and grass and wide expanses of sky and uninterrupted light. Aunt Syl and Mommi cooked all night long and we left at dawn. Cruising up the Hudson River we passed several boats and waved at strangers. A lady who I thought

I looked like with scarlet lips smiled and waved at me with her left hand. Could it be . . . ? But why did I think about her in a moment when I was happy to have an older sister who played the piano and a younger one whose Aunt-Is-Really-Her-Mother, when I had Frank Yerby, *Fairy Tales, Notes From the Underground,* and the contraband *Wonder Woman* waiting at home for me to read? Why such thoughts in a perfect moment when our ferry was gliding up the Hudson River and the August sun melted the river to gold?

At the picnic tables Mommi and Aunt Syl distributed pieces of fried chicken individually wrapped in waxed paper with our names pasted on. Daddy sprawled on a blanket in the grass, opened *The New York Daily Mirror,* and clucked his teeth in disgust as he read about the subway and bus fare rise to ten cents. Rose took out a Chinese checkers folding board and we had a quick game, while Teddie chattered to her doll in a nasal British-Bermudian accent pretending she was a Bermudian.

"Let's take a picture," said Aunt Muriel, taking out a camera and herding us together.

Daddy popped his blue suspenders and softly whistled a cornet solo as he looked into the camera.

Mommi moved nearer to Daddy, so close her body brushed his at the same time that Aunt Syl touched her yellow wide brim straw hat with her gloved fingertips. At that moment a youthful flame flared within her, then quickly went to ashes. Rose quickly applied wine-red lipstick on her full lips while Teddie stared above the camera directly into the eyes of her Aunt-Muriel-Who-Was-Really-Her-Mother. I put my hands on my hips, thrusting my flat chest forward in a sweater-girl pose, and flashed what I hoped was a Lena Horne pouty smile.

"Great Googa Mooga," chanted Aunt Muriel, trying to make us smile. Click! snapped her Brownie and in that instant, we were all together forever.

9

Thin, weak, winter morning sun glowed pale against the tall windows as the judge reentered the courtroom; his ink-black robes had a dull sheen. Seated, the judge's head bent so low over the legal papers on his desk it looked as if his neck would break. Almost as if it were painful, he slowly lifted his head and looked at me from what seemed a great distance and asked without looking at me, is that the mother?

I fought the urge to scream, Your Honor, define your terms, I don't understand the word. Instead I remained silent and stared back at him as he waited for my answer. Mother? As in a woman who gives birth to a child and leaves her never to return like May Anna did, as I am doing at this very moment? Or is the definition of a mother a woman like Mrs. Feral who nutures with one hand and destroys with the other? Which one of us deserve the title?

The idea of my own mother faded with each passing year. Ironically, through vicious and daily verbal assaults on May Anna, Mrs. Feral kept her memory alive; I vowed to defend my phantom mother. Our roles reversed, and increasingly I came to think of May Anna as my child who needed my protection against Mrs. Feral's murderous tongue.

Are you the mother? the judge repeated. The question seemed to me an accusation, for to me the word "mother" meant absence and loss.

Yes, Your Honor, I am the mother.

A diaspora

of longing. An endless

family

of legs searching for its

ancient design.

—Angela Jackson,
"The House of the Spider"

IO

We were haunted by mothers. The more I thought about my missing mother, Teddie, whose Aunt-Muriel-Was-Really-Her-Mother, lived a completely different existence. Flowing from her was what seemed to me a golden river of maternal ancestry, filled with one aunt and three uncles. As a child, Teddie knew who her real mother was but was warned never to mention it to help keep the taint of being an unwed mother away from Aunt-Muriel-Who-Is-Really-Her-Mother.

The first time I saw Teddie I was four years old and she was in the arms of her Aunt-Muriel-Who-Was-Really-Her-Mother, who was standing in our hallway under the real horseshoe that Mrs. Feral had brought from Bermuda for luck.

"I'm going to Harlem Evening High School to study typing," Aunt Muriel said. "After I land a job with the Civil Service, I plan to take back my baby," Muriel told Mrs. Feral. I tugged on her arm and stood on tiptoe trying to see our new baby. Finally, Muriel lowered her arms to my eye level so that I could see, and I fell into the universe of Teddie's big, round, luminous eyes. The light streaming from them pulled me to her, and I reached out to touch the baby. Teddie was swathed in hand-crocheted clothes and covered by a pale pink blanket sprinkled with blood-red handmade roses. Aunt Syl stood by Mommi's side inspecting

Muriel's handiwork, while Mommi inspected Muriel's black shiny pompadour wig, spiked open-toed platform shoes, and short belted red coat. Young and under five feet, she looked like a little girl in grown-up clothes.

"Her name is Theodora Miriam Louis, like in Joe," she said, handing Teddie to Mommi.

"You'll need to pay me for the extra stuff I always wind up buying. Sheltering Arms must think I'm rich . . . that measly monthly check hardly covers a morsel of food and then there's all the other things your baby will need and out of the goodness of my heart I always wind up digging into my own purse. And that's not right, is it?

"Not right a'tall," echoed her sister.

"How much?" asked Muriel resignedly.

"Should be twenty but fifteen will suffice. Every payday. Between us, of course."

"Soon as I start working," assured Muriel. As she was about to exit she turned around and said, "By the way, I don't want anyone knowing that Teddie is my child. Not even Teddie, because I'm still hoping to find a decent man. Just tell her to call me Aunt Muriel. You know, like in the cigar commercial. Muriel, the fine cigar. Why don't you come up and smoke me sometime," she laughed, and quickly shut the door behind her.

Teddie turned out to be a long-termer in foster care also. Several years later when Teddie was about seven years old, as was their habit on Sunday, streaming from various points in Harlem, Teddie's aunts and uncles congregated at our house in late afternoon. Clinging to them like heavy perfume was an afterglow of Harlem streets. They self-consciously fidgeted on the unyielding plastic covers of our living room as they unsuccessfuly tried to mask the aura of rent parties, Saturday night functions, and low-down gut-bucket blues that engulfed them.

The first to arrive was Muriel's youngest brother, Uncle Bip-Bam-Boom the punch-drunk, would be-fighter who acquired his name because that was the sound (he said) his boxing gloves made against his opponent's jaws. His problem was that somehow he was the one that always went down for the count. Nevertheless, Uncle Bip-Bam-Boom was a source of hope for the Louis family. As a boxer he had a chance of making something out of himself.

As Uncle Bip-Bam-Boom became more punch-drunk, he supported himself by trying to become an expert light-finger. No better thief than he was a boxer, he was always "away" for periods of time. His face bore the brunt of his confrontations in the ring and in jail. His soft-spoken, polite and gentle manner belied the violence of his life. In anticipation of a visit from him, Mommi would rush around the apartment removing all valuables from sight, declaring, "Nail everything down to the ground. Bip-Bam-Boom is on his way."

"Go buy a house," he laughingly commanded Teddie and me, letting us pick gleaming new pennies from his upturned palm as soon as he entered our apartment.

Trying not to stare at his low left eye and then at the high right one, we followed him down the hallway, into our living room as he danced from side to side, boxing invisible opponents. No sooner had he settled in a plastic corner on the couch than there was a knock, a ring, and a mellifluous "open the door, Richard, Richard, why don't you open dat door?" coming from Aunt Queenie.

"Sweets for the sweeties," purred Aunt Queenie, who was always loaded. As soon as she stepped over our threshold, she offered Teddie and me bags of penny, valentine, heart-shaped pastel-colored candy with "will you be mine" written in red. Raspy voiced with the Louis trademark of big luminous moon eyes, I thought Aunt Queenie, with her huge eyes, marcelled hair, and bright red bow mouth, looked like Jean Harlow in the old silent films. Easing on in behind her was her male "friend," who changed weekly. After paying their respects to Mommi and Aunt Syl, both would join Uncle Bip-Bam-Boom and sit on the couch in a serene, alcoholic haze.

Uncle Georges, as usual, arrived after Uncle Boom. Georges was the refined one of the Louis clan. Prim and proper, he wore a slanted beret, tried to grow a beard, studied French, added an "s" to the end of his name for a touch of class, and played the violin. As we followed him down the hall to the living room, Teddie and I called him a "sissy" and giggled at his baggy, rumpled clothing.

Uncle Georges took his usual seat opposite tipsy Aunt Queenie and her latest paramour, and watched Uncle Bip-Bam-Boom quietly bobbing, weaving, and ducking phantom blows to his head. Uncle Georges just rolled his eyes as he always did and mournfully clucked, "Common, common, just plain common."

The next to appear was Uncle Eddie-Sam, my favorite. Winter or summer, he would arrive, dapper in a jauntily tipped white fedora, white suit, and walking stick to match, and gleaming white patent leather shoes. He would always audaciously attempt to involve Mommi in his latest business venture.

"This is it, my ship has finally come in, Mrs. Feral," he said, waving some membership cards in front of her.

"Looks like your ship has been in a while," Mommi retorted, eyeing his attire. "And you been keeping the cargo all to yourself."

"Got's to keep the chippie's playground looking sharp," said Uncle Eddie-Sam, explaining his prosperous looking appearance.

"For someone who is broke all the time, you look expensive."

"Now Mrs. Feral, I know you are a businesswoman. Join my Pyramid Club. In a few weeks, when your name gets to the top, you'll have enough for a down payment for a house in St. Albans, Long Island."

"I'm not a gambler."

"You play the numbers everyday."

"That's different. Everyone plays the numbers."

"Policy is old-fashioned. White folks taking over. Now everyone joining the Pyramid Clubs."

"Not everyone," said Mommi.

"That's what's wrong with us. No economic vision. Invest with me instead of putting it in a bank. In a few weeks you will be paid dividends from money provided by the investors that come after you. Believe me, this thing is growing and I'm offering it to you, Mrs. Feral, because I know you are a capitalist at heart. Everyone is doing it."

"Not everyone," repeated Mommi with finality, "not me."

Their visit with Teddie officially began as Aunt Muriel, always the last to arrive, in a new, carefully curled wig, glanced around our living room, silently took attendance.

> *"If I go to church on Sunday*
> *And cabaret all day Monday*
> *Ain't nobody's business if I do."*

Muriel had just purchased some 45's from Rainbow's and we were all dancing to the voice warbling from the Victrola.

"Oh that woman's singing makes me feel soooooo unnecessary," squealed Aunt Queenie delightedly, rolling her buttocks in time with the music.

"Ahhhh baby come to Daddy, c'mon to Daddy daddy!" gurgled Uncle Eddie-Sam to the vinyl Billie as he stuck out his behind and did the fish and grind, hugging the wide victrola as if it was a woman. Uncle Bip-Bam-Boom grinned lopsidedly as Teddie and I did the ballroom strut like white folks in the movies. Muriel snickered at Mommi's disapproving looks, while Uncle Georges watched glumly and involuntarily tapped his foot now and then as he slyly swayed to the music.

"Enough of that liquor house, low gut, trashy singing. Turn her off, " ordered Mommi.

"That's Lady Day," objected Muriel.

"Lady? Sounds like a cat to me," countered Mommi.

"Alley cat. A common alley cat," said Uncle Georges, superior to us in his agreement with Mommi.

"YeeeeeOw. A sick common alley cat. Yeeow," Mommi repeated the high nasal sound that was supposed to be an imitation of Billie. In one deft movement she lifted up the needle, removed the record, and closed the top of the victrola with a final thud.

"Hells bells," muttered Aunt Muriel audibly under her breath for all to hear.

"Street language goes with that street music I just turned off."

I sprawled out on the rug beside her trying to pretend to ignore the tension flying around the room.

"Let's see how good you write your name," Aunt Muriel challenged Teddie in an effort to change the atmosphere. Teddie took the thick piece of blue chalk and the wooden-framed blackboard with an abacus of green, red, and yellow wooden balls on top. Kneeling on the carpet next to her daughter, Aunt Muriel watched as Teddie slowly formed the letters of her first name.

"Good," she said, passing the blackboard around the room so her brothers and sister could admire their niece's chalk blue inscription of "Theodora."

"Now, write our last name." The room was silent except for the sound of Teddie's chalk against her blackboard. Everyone savored the silence, glad to have escaped the previous threatening hostilities.

"Noooo," exclaimed Muriel, snatching the blackboard from Teddie and hurling it across the room. The multicolored wooden balls filled the room with a hollow rattle. Muriel began a sudden wheezing.

"I'll be damn," observed Uncle Eddie-Sam as he picked up the blackboard. He held it high for all to see where Teddie had written her last name as "Feral" in wavy blue letters. "I'll be goddam—"

"Not in my house you won't," said Mommi. "Save that for the gutter!"

"Odd's farts! Great Googa Mooga!" yelled Uncle Georges, looking at what Teddie had scrawled.

"Teddie, you are old enough to know your family name," said Uncle Eddie-Sam. "We may be some loose, low, Harlem niggers from the South," he said, looking at Mommi, "but we stick together and our name is Louis, like in Joe. Now you write it!"

Teddie screamed and ran to Mommi. Muriel wheezed, and gasped for air and ran for a glass of water.

"No Feral," grunted Uncle Bip, shadow boxing and punching his family name in the air.

"L," he yelled, jabbing and feinting.

"O," he gave a right punch, then a left.

"U," he stabbed the air several times.

"I," bobbing and weaving.

"S," an uppercut into the thin air.

Finished, he stood still, peered at Teddie, and said "Louis like in Joe," and did some fancy footwork until Mommi said, "What I want to know from you is why don't you win a fight, join the army, or stay in jail?"

Teddie started yelping in Mommi's arms.

"Come to me," Aunt-Muriel-Who-Was-Really-Her mother said faintly.

"You're not my mother," sobbed Teddie to Muriel.

Muriel turned to Mommi and in between her deep wheezes, sputtered, "Who taught her that her name was Feral?"

"What do you expect when you try to cover her up like a bald head?"

Grabbing Teddie, Aunt Muriel said, "Your name is Louis, not Feral."

"No," said Teddie furiously pulling away from her.

"Ahhhggghhg!" moaned Aunt Muriel, ripping off her wig and hurling it to the floor. It lay on the rug like an inert animal, its long thick black curls stiff and glossy. We all gaped at her short, kinky hair for the first time.

"Look at me," gasped Aunt Muriel with a thick voice with long gasps for air in between. "I ain't got no hair, I don't have a husband, but I got you. You hear me girl," she demanded of Teddie, hardly able to catch her breath. "You're mine so you look at me. Look at your mother!"

"You awake?" breathed Teddie in the dark, later that night in our room.

"You betta sleep, girl."

"Let's pretend," begged Teddie. And then our voices took on a conspiratorial hush hush with cadences of wishes as we turned into Wonder Woman flying around in a bathing suit, and Esther Williams ballet dancing in the water and Sonja Henie gliding across lakes of ice.

"You know what?" asked Teddie suddenly.

"Chicken butt. That's what."

"C'mon, I'm serious."

"Glad to meet you serious, I'm mysterious."

"Stop playing around. Don't tell Mommi."

"About what."

"You know. That Aunt Muriel is really my mother. I knew it all along. Don't tell Mommi I said that. I don't want her to be mad at me."

"She's not mad at you. She's mad at me. She says I'm a bad influence on you."

"So what? She always says that."

"I know. I don't care."

"Is your mother coming for you?"

"Who? May Anna? I think she forgot."

"You should be glad."

"Why?"

"Since you don't know who your real mother is you can be anything you want. You could be a fairy princess. Or something. I kinda liked being a Bermudian."

"Why?"

"Cause, they are better than even West Indians and they know who their mothers are. Not like us."

"But Teddie, Aunt Muriel really *is* your mother."

"I know. What can I do? I'm only a kid."

"Go to sleep."

"Are we still sisters?"

"Of course."

"Mothers don't have anything to do with that, right?"

"Right."

"Tell Rose," Teddie murmured and fell fast asleep.

—

Aunt-Muriel-Who-Was-Really-Her-Mother dropped dead the day after. The asthmatic wheezing that began when she took off her wig, exposed her short kinky hair, and publicly claimed Teddie as her daughter never stopped. She never did catch her breath again, and in the morning her landlady found her cold in her room. Mrs. Feral took charge of all the arrangements, and the wake was held at our house. Aunt Queenie, Uncle Bip-Bam-Boom, Georges, and Uncle Eddie-Sam, their faces rubbery with tears, sat around and drank rum and Coke and ate potato salad and fish cakes and chicken and peas and rice and cornbread and talked about the old days when they first came to New York.

"Some folks, FOB, fresh off the bus, coming from the South, landed in Jersey by accident. The driver said 'Newark' and they thought it was New York," Uncle Eddie-Sam laughed.

"When we first came to New York the colored lived in Thompson Street what was called Little Africa. When the colored moved to the Tenderloin district on the West Side in the sixties they sang

Got too much chuck
Want a piece of the tenderloin.

and then we just kept being pushed further and further uptown where the whites tried their best to keep us out of Harlem." I tried to imagine white folks living in Harlem as he continued to talk almost as if he were afraid of being silent.

"I got another song.

Silver and Gold
Silver and Gold
I'm going to Panama
To dig a Canal hole
Silver and Gold
Silver and Gold

"That ain't no song, that's a fact. Back in nineteen and eleven I was working the Panama Canal. They had two payrolls, a white and a black one, gold and silver. Gold was $120.00 a month. Silver was $40.00. When they could tell the difference they put American Negroes on the 'Nigger Gold' roll, $80.00, and the West Indian on the silver and kept us fighting.

"But some of us helped the West Indians to pass. My buddy, Clive, from Barbados, was passing as a Geechee so he could get some 'nigger gold.' Clive mastered funny mumbo jumbo with a lot of 'nassuh' and 'massuh' thrown in. Worked fine until one day the foreman called Clive a 'nigger.' Well, Clive drew his short self up and said in full Barbadian English, 'I am a British subject and I will write my king about your churlish behavior.'"

Uncle Eddie-Sam threw his head so far back his eyes were parallel to the ceiling and he laughed in rhythm. Beginning at the top of the scale in a high falsetto and kicking one leg straight out in front of him, his voice and his back got lower with each convulsive gasp until he finished on a low bass note, bent all the way over, clutching his stomach, his head bobbing up and down, his forehead touching the floor in what could easily be mistaken for a posture of prayer. It was difficult to tell whether he was laughing or sobbing but I did know that this was his way of mourning.

—

The next week Mommi announced that she felt that she deserved the five thousand dollars insurance money that Muriel left Teddie. After all she had done for Muriel, taking care of Teddie out of the goodness of her heart, no one was better entitled to the money.

Teddie agreed and was overjoyed when her foster mother bought her a brand new bicycle with the insurance money. Teddie did not go to Aunt-Muriel-Who-Was-Really-Her-Mother's funeral, but there was a large heart-shaped wreath of white roses bought with a card signed in Mommi's handwriting, Rest In Peace, From Your Loving Niece, Theodora Feral.

Many years later, after I had given Kelvin away for adoption, I stood at her deathbed in Harlem Hospital and saw that Teddie still had the same bright eyes she had when I stood on tiptoe to peek at her for the first time when she lay in Aunt-Muriel-Who-Was-Really-Her-Mother's arms. Breast cancer, alcohol, violent men, poverty, had not dimmed the steady and shining light that streamed from her eyes. They were still bright even though her five children surrounded her deathbed in confusion and anger because I had revealed to them that Mommi was not Teddie's real mother and that her name was Theodora Louis and not Feral. It was the first time they had ever heard about their grandmother, Aunt-Muriel-Who-Was-Really-Her-Mother. Teddie still had the same high forehead, though it was hot with fever, the same golden brown complexion, though now dulled with morphine and disease, and the same pug nose, as if someone stuck it on as an afterthought.

When she opened her eyes and recited as if I were a stranger, "I was born in Bermuda and my name is Theodora Feral," I replied, "Your name is Theodora Miriam Louis, like in Joe, and your kids have a right to know the truth about themselves, it's time you stop lying."

"No," said Teddie wearily, as she took a long look at me and, with great effort, lifted her fingers to touch the small keloid in the center of my right eyebrow where Mommi's iron cord bit me years ago, saying, "You stood up to her. You were the only one. I can still see that iron cord whooshing through the air. I can still hear you hollering."

"Why can't you tell your kids about your own mother? Tell them who their real grandmother was. Tell them about Aunt Muriel."

"Why? It gives them a lift to think their Grandmother was a high-tone Bermudian woman with a house in Springfield Gardens—"

"—earned off the backs of us foster children," I interrupted as I removed her hand from my face, thinking about the days when we pretended that we were Mrs. Feral's real children and not merely her foster charges. We wanted to pretend that we were the daughters in her high-class Bermudian family instead of illegitimate offspring of Southern peasants, that we bore her name instead of our own. Sometimes Mommi let us pretend and promised us she wouldn't tell anybody who we really were. But everyone knew our public secret and called us the make believe sisters with the pretend last names.

"Pretending ain't lying and lots of times the truth ain't what's real," Teddie gasped, closing her eyes suddenly as if I were not standing there. Only death could cut off her glow and shut down her persistent inner humor.

And when she stopped breathing, I knew our past was like glittering mica strewn and imbedded in the Harlem concrete, only discernable by the most far-seeing eye.

II

Kelvin, I am glad that you're born a man. I hope you're the sort of man I would like to be. A man who knows the heart and brain has no sex; a man who acknowledges no limits to his being in the world. A man who behaves as if he is a god, kind to the weak, fierce to the arrogant, generous to those who love you, ruthless to those who would order you around. A man who does not let the injustice against him make him rabid. For yes, my boy, you will have to struggle. They will try to humiliate you, enslave you, and demand that you comply in their acts of mayhem and bondage. They will give you a uniform with orders to kill or be killed. A prison cell with your name awaits. They will try to deny your humanity and judge you by your tailpiece in front. Whenever you take pride in yourself you will be ridiculed. When you build something they will tear it down. They will rob you. Their sons and daughters will benefit from their fathers' plunders but will not take responsibility for their ancestors' crimes, while your children and grandchildren will start out in life at point zero with nothing handed down but the life within them. Nothing, except hope.

I am awed by the mystery of life. How can it be that I, who know nothing of men, can bear a son? How is it possible that I can pass life on in the the body and spirit of a male child when in my own life males are, if not menacing, then like my foster father, an impenetrable and receding shadow?

12

"Here comes my Daddy," I would yell as his felt hat high above the other heads in the street and broad shoulders turned in from Lenox Avenue and headed down the block. Bounding down the stairs two at a time I would run to meet him, take his hand, and walk with him, the silent Daddy who barely spoke, who now whistled like he was playing his cornet. Under his arm would be a folded *World Telegram and Sun* and in his frayed pockets might be a prize from a Cracker Jack box or a new pink Spaldeen.

He lived in an atmosphere that excluded males, unable to invade the psychic fortress the two sisters erected against him. His tall frame and broad shoulders were always slightly hunched over as if he was afraid of blocking someone's sight line. His affability had nothing to do with good-naturedness. He mastered the smile, the grin, the surface pleasantness. Always deferential, he covered his hand with his mouth whenever a loud laugh escaped from him, avoided direct eye contact with anyone, and always spoke with a creeping plaintiveness in his voice.

I pretended that he was my silent ally. Sometimes I imagined that in the middle of a whipping through my tears I saw him winking at me. I made myself believe this silent man was just biding his time, waiting for the day when he would rise to my defense and stop his wife's punishing hand in midair. But that was before the day he was adamant in his refusal to change his church membership and said in his wavering voice, "Stop it Winnie, you confounded woman, all you do is try to make me into a cow's udder," slammed the door, and stormed out, and I followed him.

"Make haste," were the only words he said that acknowledged my presence as we descended the steps into Mount Morris Park. Breathless from trying to keep up with his long strides, I gloried in his long legs, his broad shoulders, his wide-brim gray felt hat worn in all seasons. We always took the same route through the seesaws, sliding boards, monkey climbers, and swings, past the suspicious park matron ever ready for trouble who positioned herself in front of the doorless toilets in the girls' bathroom, past the aged summer men in suspenders, caps, and overcoats playing their ongoing game of checkers, and up, up the steep, narrow, winding stairs to the old bell tower.

Long, round, sonorous whistles gusted from Daddy's mouth, falling on top of one another, curling like the spiral steps as we climbed up the rocky cliff. When we reached the top he became silent. Seated on the iron benches he pulled out his constant companion, a black-covered Bible with pages edged in red. A long silent cast iron bell grownups said was once rung to announce a fire hung gloomily in front of us. Daddy was weeping now but making no sound. Only his broad shoulders twitched slightly. He would sigh now and then, make a light feathery sound, and clack his teeth. He clutched his Bible and prayed without moving his lips. I sensed he forgot that I was there and I sat still not daring to look directly at him.

When we got back Mommi was waiting for us.

"What were you two doing in the park till way past dark?" she screamed as soon as we stepped into the house and she slammed the door behind us. Following us down the long hallway, she continued screaming and looking at me but really talking to Daddy.

"Why were you in the park till way past dark. I know I've nur-
tured a monster," she screamed, lunged for me, and smacked my
face. "I *know* what's on your mind and you better not!"

My face stinging, I looked at Daddy, appealing to him silently.
Now is the time, Daddy. Do Something! Say Something! Cut off
her hands! Shut her mouth! Knock her teeth down her throat!
Leave her and take me with you! Anything to stop those hateful
words! Instead he stood still, stunned, and when he recovered he
retreated to his bedroom and closed the door without a word.
Mommi and Aunt Syl were left to enjoy long intimate hours together. Aunt Syl's bedroom door was left open and I could see
them: Mommi getting dressed and Aunt Syl helping her into her
corset, talking and smiling.

From that day on I knew Daddy, or at least the idea of him, was
lost to me forever. He became more silent, and we both lived in
that apartment with Mommi's sly accusation hovering in our
memories. Her words, only half understood then, became clearer
with each passing year and filled me with a searing, primal shame.
I never looked at him again, and Daddy began to disappear right
before our eyes. The only thing he was vocal about was his religion and his refusal to attend Mommi's elite and somber Episco-
palian church with the rest of us. Being the deacon of a small,
storefront church, the Holiness Tabernacle, Temple, Refuge, and
Sanctuary of the Spiritual Baptists on Lenox Avenue and 115th
Street, whose congregation was shouting, stomping, Southern
Negroes, did not bring Daddy family admiration. Six days a week
he arose at three A.M. to go to New Jersey to a General Motors
plant where he would stoke the furnace, but he lived for the Sundays when as deacon he would conduct the evening service.

I always wondered how Daddy looked, standing in front of a
congregation, and what was the message in the sermons he
preached. One day, not long after our last walk in Mount Morris
Park, I followed him to church one Sunday.

—

The Sunday sidewalks gleamed with church going-folks in their once-a-week clothes. The women sparkled in brightly colored hats with gloves, shoes, and pocketbooks to match. Grandmothers fiercely clutched the hands of young boy children as if afraid they would fly away if they relaxed their grip. Old men, stiff-backed in dark suits and red paper carnations in their lapels, teenage boys, clumped together, dutifully walked with their families, erect under their oldsters' gaze, trying not to dip forward, rotate their shoulders and weave their bodies from side to side in their hep weekday walk. Rolling organs and pealing choir voices, carillon bells in lofty bell towers, and rhythmic tambourines and drums from storefront temples beckoning their respective congregations, commingled in the Harlem Sunday morning air and beat back the street people on Lenox Avenue for the moment. Dark women's faces peppered with puffy shiny scars, pointed two-tone shoes and bright peg-leg pants that grew on the corners in front of the bars, and sibilant "sssssssssts" of white men sliding up and down the streets in cars holding dollar bills in the air hissing for women all vanished during Sunday morning church services. Walking toward daddy's church instead of Sunday School, the thought of yet another illicit church experience pleased me. Church hopping was a favorite pastime among us girls, a subterfuge used when all other social activities were banned. I had attended the Black Jews Shabbat on Friday, the Stations of the Cross at Lent, Mount Olivet Baptist Church and the sanctified storefronts in the evening lots of times with Fat Helen. The storefront services were the most exciting. On entering the small one-room churches, the sight of the nurse-saints in white uniforms standing by with smelling salts, in anticipation for those who would be slain in the Spirit, filled me with delicious terror; the sight of a soul possessed filled me with a fear I was ashamed to feel. There was no music like their music: the high piano melody feeding the drum's deep resonance, the insistent drumbeat pushing human bodies to sway in unison, voices, trembling with emotion, relishing the notes, savoring the tune, caressing the words. The preacher was not a man but a dancing, moaning, exulting force, wildly tossing his congregation's emotions about on the waves of his tumultuous voice.

I hoped Daddy's church would be like that, I thought as I paused for a moment, watching The Moor, a midnight blue man, swathed in an orange robe and turban encrusted with rhinestones, stars, and crescents, explaining the meanings of the pink chalk pyramids, circles, stars, and numbers he had drawn on the sidewalks.

"Aw forget the mysti mojo, just tell us what the digit's gonna be today, tell us what figure to play, I need to hit the number," a man in the crowd called out.

Turning my back on the crowd's laughter, I quickly passed an evicted woman sitting on her sofa wearing a bathrobe and a hat, a soft black velvet beret with a long lacquered black feather, watching three children romp through her pots and pans and fling her brassieres to a cloudless sky.

—

Blond, blue-eyed, rose-lipped Jesus cuddles fat lambs and open Bibles float on clouds on the stained windows of Daddy's Holiness Tabernacle one flight over Jackson's ABC Auto School, Notary Public, and Photo Studio, Inc. But why is the door closed and the church in total darkness? Am I too early? No matter, I'll just stand and bounce my brand new Spaldeen and watch folks gather in front of the church and fellowship with one another before they file inside.

"One Eat a Plum put your right foot over one." *I love the way my skinny brown legs flash over the rubber ball as it kisses the sidewalk and springs back into my hands only to be pushed back to the ground again and*

"Two touch your shoe put your right foot over two." *Nobody's here yet but I know Daddy's inside.*

"Five step aside . . . put your right" . . . *Something is wrong.*

"Seven, go to" . . . N*obody's here yet but when I get to twelve everybody should be here.*

"Eight shut the gate." *He can't preach to an empty church. Where is everybody?*

"Ten," *I'm not supposed to be here. I can't let Daddy see me.*

"Ele . . ." *I'm going inside. I know he's in there.*

In the empty room I slipped into one of the rows of wooden chairs that began to take shape in the blackness and I sat on it, squeezing the ball in my pocket for courage. Electric light bulbs on the rim of a huge pine cross were suddenly lit as Deacon Feral stepped up to his pulpit and faced his phantom congregation with unseeing eyes. Carrying his worn Bible, he raised his right hand in benediction. In a reedy voice, without weight, he began.

"From the life of Job, I take my text and I take my time." Without the traditional response "yes, Preach . . . take your time . . . take your tiiiiiiime!" his words fell flat in the deep emptiness. "Job," he continued, "chewed water. Yes, I said and I'll say it again. Job, God's servant had to chew water." He stood still for a minute looking into the empty darkness and then listening to the emptiness he began:

> I feeeeel
> Your scornful eyes
> And I hear
> Your mockful tongues
> But I'm asking you Church,
> O don't cha know,
> My gentle ain't weak
> My quiet ain't calm
> My meek ain't mild
> My hold back ain't fear?

Believe me Church,
My tears are
Chewed water
Flowing from
Ancient,
Unceasing streams
Sorrow thick
Pain bitten
Bones in the eye
Swallowed whole
Indigestible
O! My Lord.

Raising his hands, he began playing his invisible cornet while whistling "Onward Christian Soldiers," whistling in perfect pitch, strong, lusty, long, extended notes billowing on one another higher and higher. Then Daddy fell down on his knees, his arms extended in crucifixion posture at the bottom of the electric cross.

"O LORD. TELL SATAN, TELL GOD, I AM ONLY A MAN. SEE, SEE."

His face twisted, he began touching himself all over screaming, "SEE MY EYES, SEE MY EARS, SEE MY NOSE," and growing angry he continued his journey downward on his body, his fingers now holding his legs screaming, "SEE MY LEGS SATAN TELL GOD YOU GOD SATAN, GOD, SEE MY—"

I fled, leaving him in mid-sentence. The pink ball in my pocket fell out and rolled to the front of the small church. I didn't care. I had attended Sunday School too long not to know what happened to those who saw their father naked. Even though Daddy's body was not unclothed in his empty church, I knew I had seen something not meant for my eyes.

That evening, when he returned, as was his habit, Daddy put some money in Mommi's straw basket on the kitchen table. It was, he said, the proceeds from the collection plate he had passed after his sermon. Some crumpled up dollar bills and lots of loose change.

13

Langston Hughes was my father. In the *Amsterdam News* a picture
of the writer revealed to me that he and Mr. Feral shared a melancholy gaze fixed on a vision in a far-away horizon; both men had a
spirit of solitude wrapped in a seemingly imperturbable halo of
languor. But rage and pain seethed in Mr. Hughes's words, while
my foster father took things quietly although he felt them deeply.
I claimed the poet as my one true ancestor. Sitting in my fourth-
grade class listening to Miss Matlin read his poems, I was convinced that they were his secret codes and private messages to me.
Everytime I went outdoors I ran into Miss Susanna Jones.

> *When Susanna Jones wears red*
> *A queen from some time-dead Egyptian night*
> *Walks again*

In my classroom, I laughed, looking at her red shoes, red dress,
and red lips, loving how Susanna Jones's deep brown flesh glowed
darker in the redness. In the spaces that connected my poet
father's words about Susanna Jones, I found my own mother.

As I turned the page, Miss Matlin's creamy contralto nuzzled
against my ears. "Langston Hughes is the Shakespeare of Harlem."

Some folks said that the only reason she talked this way was because she was a Communist who refused teaching assignments in

white neighborhoods to teach in Harlem. Others said she only did so because she was really a light-skinned colored woman. I didn't know what to believe but I knew that some folks had a bad habit of making everybody they liked colored whether they were or not.

"You can be a teacher and stand behind my desk one day," Miss Matlin used to say, although we had never seen a black teacher. I loved watching her standing in front of the classroom, the sun from the window igniting her long brown hair golden, her voice flaming, her pockmarked face suddenly beautiful as she talked about "freedom and equality for the Negro People." Later on in the beginning of 1948 when she was dismissed by the Board of Education for "radical activities," I knew it was because she praised men like Paul Robeson, Ben Davis, and Langston Hughes, as she was doing right now.

"He is the bard, the Shakespeare of Harlem," she said, holding the book high above her head and pointing to the famous poet with the same last name as mine.

"He is the father," she said looking straight at me, "of all of us who celebrate Harlem."

At the first tremor of the three o'clock bell I bolted from my seat and ran all the way to 123rd Street to the small public library facing Mount Morris Park. The library had been a small mansion, with marble stairs and a winding staircase with gleaming brass banisters that led up to the children's reading room on the second floor. The bowed heads of the readers, the tall rectangle windows with light streaming into the huge room, and the beatific manner of the librarians (those angels of literature) as they guided me from book to book always filled me with reverence whenever I entered.

"Langston Hughes," the librarian smiled at my book and then at me at the checkout counter. Handing me the book she said in a sweet voice full of pride, "The Shakespeare of Harlem. Do you know he lives right around the corner on 127th Street?"

With his books under my arm, I ran to find my father's house.

A wizened, leathery-faced woman wearing a thick cotton orange stocking cap and slippers sat wide-legged on a brownstone step and watched me serenely as I scurried down 127th Street.

"Where can I find him? Which house is his?" I asked her as if we had been carrying on a conversation.

"Gal?"

"Mr. Hughes, the poet."

"Oh. Him." She squinted her eyes, studying me, and then removing the pipe she was sucking on and jerking her head to the right she said, "Dyar, h'it."

It was just one of an entire block of reddish brownstones with green window boxes overflowing with red and white geraniums. Did he have other children? Did I look like them? Did he have a wife? Was he home? I was feverish with these thoughts when magically the door opened and a dapper, tan man with wavy hair and a hint of a smile in his sad eyes appeared.

"Daughter," he said, instantly recognizing me. "Sent for you yesterday and here you come today. Come on in."

I stepped into my father's house. He tilted my head back, inspecting my face and without words I followed him up the stairs. In his study, he sat at his desk and reached for an ink pen and a large scratch pad. Once in a while he would gaze at me and then write on the blue-lined yellow pad in bright green ink. I watched him scribble words that would become a famous poem. Finally, Papa (for that is what I would call him) stopped writing, and lifted his head saying, "You look like May Anna," but just as I was about to ask him where my mother was the old woman scratched her stocking cap and growled at me, "Go long home, gal, scoot! Can't you see it's gettin dark. Y'bin switchin up and down dat block like you practicing for a parade. Scoot home I say."

Overhead the sky growled as if in agreement. Two rain-streaked, ashy brown legs with drooping socks propelled me forward and a sudden vicious rain pour whipped me homeward.

14

In that endless morning, in order to escape the cold, unseeing legal gaze, the cries of a soon to be gone forever baby, the social worker seated beside me full of sincere missionary pity, the uncomfortable wooden benches, the flat air and pale, urine-colored winter sun trickling through the courtroom windows and the intimidation I felt whenever I was below 110th Street, I recalled the joy of a Harlem parade on a Saturday afternoon, the feathers, the faraway music gathering force as it grew near. Always, at the first hint of music, reality was suspended as I ran to dive into the sound. Hurry, hurry, I don't want to miss the beginning, I don't want to miss Ancestor Gold Sky on top of his dancing, gleaming white horse.

15

Ancestor Gold Sky lifts a long yellow fingernail and points upward. There are feathers everywhere. The streets are filled with
dancing feet. Perched on top of his white horse, the patriarch's ancient eyes reflect the white sky. The crowd cheers as the white
horse canters in a circle. A soft wind blows. His back is rigid. His
eyes swim across the heavens. His arm, a knotted branch, rests in
midair as a gold fingernail dips, rises, and flashes in sunlight, as
his white horse's hooves lift up high and clip-clop a liquid sound
against the hot asphalt.

Now Ancestor Gold Sky drops his hand and gently pulls the
white horse's reins. His steed high-steps gracefully to the beat of
the oncoming brass bands. Oom m pah pppahhh. On the sidewalk grown-up footsteps slyly slip into a high step. Feathers are
everywhere. Headdresses of white and red quills sway in the air.
Ancestor Gold Sky's eyes return to the crowd. His yellow suit is
the color of the July midday sun. He is The Leader. The Opener.
The marching bands keep a respectful distance behind him but on
they come. Racing down flights of stairs, pouring out of storefronts, folks stream forth from every street and join the parade.
On the beat. Left, right, right, left. Ooom Phhhaa.

People, music, feathers are everywhere. Feathers wave and waft
in windless summer air and I am following this parade. White

horse hooves lift high in the air like a prancing girl. A drum majorette's gleaming white boots high step to the brass band beat. She struts and kicks and twirls a baton encrusted with sequins. A Spanish man's Aztec face floats high above us on a flatbed truck as he holds aloft his tambourine, its small brass discs flashing in the sun.

Far ahead, Ancestor Gold Sky becomes a speck in the distance as the parade bursts into bloom. The frilly floppy plummage of bright feathery skirts swing and sway. Everywhere folks are dancing in the street.

A drum majorette prances on her toes, her white boots like horses' hooves.

Ommm pah ommm pah Phhaaaa.

A toddler jigs on a man's shoulders. Dancing in the streets. Traveling up his right side and down his left, high above us on his moving truck the Spanish man rhythmically smacks his body fast and furious with his tambourine. Now he holds it in the air and shakes its bells. Oola! he exults.

Oom pahhh ooom pahhh oom pah.

In all the houses folks forget what they are doing and fly into the street from every direction. Ooom pah om pahhh. Thick brass serpentine tubas coil around musicians' necks and growl and purr, growl and purr.

Ooomm Phah Oom Phaaa Oom Phaaaa.

Gleaming tubas crouch low on the ground. Kick their feet. And slide. Left. Right. A man in a wheelchair wheels. Left. Right. On the beat. The joy of dancing in the streets.

The cymbalists leap into the air with each clang! of their brass discs. Clang! Clang! Clang! Clang! Clang! Clang! The rapture of dancing.

The Elks, The Sons and Daughters of, The Bermuda Benevolent Society, The Social and Pleasure Union of, The Sistren and Brethren of, The Burial and Aid Committee of, The Ethiopian Hebrews, The Coptic Moors, Abbysinian Baptists, Egyptian Nubians stream forth from every block and join the parade. On the beat. Left right right left. Ooom phaa phaaa phaa.

The parade engulfs me and feathers sway in the summer air. Here comes the sanctys, murmurs a voice as the white-robed women from a Pentecostal church on 137th Street fall in line, automatically picking up the beat, and I am surrounded by the parade. Ooom phhh oom PhhahhhPooom Phhh. At 138th Street, ancient Garveyites step stiffly to the brass band's beat. The music enters me. The rhythm washes me. I want this parade in me forever.

Little boys become jumping beans. They bend low, stretch out flat on the ground, twitch around and leap high. They dance on top of cars. They scuttle to the top of lamposts and wriggle to the drumbeats. Girls swing round behinds round and round. Girls are having dance-offs on the sidewalks. Dancing in the street. And there are feathers everywhere. Indian feathers. African feathers. Skirts of feathers. Crowns of feathers. Light feathers, bright feathers, heavy feathers, dark feathers. I push through crowds and skip along besides the music and the marchers.

A feather floats in the air and outlines a halo above my head. The parade stops. Silence. We are now at 125th Street and Lenox Avenue and the feather above me lingers a while before settling on my bare scalp right where I part my hair. An ancient general of some mythic army, stiff with age and heavy medals with an unsheathed saber hanging loosely at his waist, is helped up to an impromptu dais. He does battle with his loose false teeth as he excitedly declares

> In the trrrrrradition!
> . Of St. Patty's Day for the Irrrrrrrrish!
> Columbus Day for the Italians
> Pulaski Day for the Poles!
> Grrrrrreek Independence day for the
> Greeeks!
> We pay trrribute to our Ancestooorrrs!

Homage to ourrrrrselves!
And salute Harrrrrrrrlem!

The bands start up again. The marchers pick up their feet and
turn toward Seventh Avenue. Flight and Freedom. That's what
feathers mean. I know because my fourth grade teacher at P.S. 184
told me so and I want this music, this color, this jubilance, this
day in me forever.

As we pass Thom McCann's shoe store, large cardboard signs
on long wooden sticks are lifted and sway high above the
marcher's heads like ominous paper birds. DON'T BUY WHERE YOU
CAN'T WORK. Left. Right. Left. Right. Left. Right Strut. Bend
strut bend strut strut strut. On Seventh Avenue we are in front of
the gold lettering of F. W. Woolworth 5 and 10. NO BLACK CLERKS
NO BLACK MONEY. Ooomphha oom phhha oom phha. As we pass
Busch Credit Jewelers the signs float higher. ONLY A FOOL SPENDS
MONEY WHERE HE IS NOT WANTED. Ooooom Phhhh Phhhha!
Plink plank plink plank. Steel band and brass band respond to
each other. Blumstein's Department Store. The air is thick with
ominous cardboard birds.WHY ARE THERE NO BLACK CLERKS IN
HARLEM STORES? THE BLACK HAND THAT EARNS IS THE BLACK
HAND THAT BUYS. NO BLACK LABOR NO GREEN BLACK MONEY. The
birds rise higher and higher. They sing their silent songs and float
noiselessly on sticks raised in the air.

As we pass the window of Howard's Clothing Store, which dis-
plays apricot zoot suits on pink mannequins, the birds rise higher
and silently sing DONT BUY WHERE YOU CAN'T TRY ON! This brilliant feather on my head is red and black and green.

Somewhere someone plays a piccolo.

The sparkle of Herbert's Home of Blue White Diamonds sign
glares at us as we strut in 3/4 time. A cardboard bird carried by the
small dark man next next to me sings 25 YEARS IN HARLEM AND
NOT EVEN A JANITOR. On Eighth Avenue policemen in riot gear
greet the parade in front of Weisbecker Markets. What is this, a

parade or a protest demonstration? You have no registered route. A parade permit was not purchased. Your music is a public nuisance. Your signs are Communist propaganda. You have no license. You people are illegal.

Waves of music. Steel pan and brass bands. Oom pahh pahh, pling plinnk plinnnk. Cardboard birds floating in the sky. A feather that has floated through the air rests in the crossroads of my scalp. Ancestor Gold Sky turns his horse around and faces the procession. He lifts his arms. Why is that old lunatic on top of a horse waving his hand in the air, wonders a young white policeman. All the bands raise their instruments along with Ancestor Gold Sky. Bullets of sunlight dart from them. Tambourine man flashes jangling golden discs to the heavens. All arms are raised in the air.

There is a feather in my hair.

16

In Harlem, in 1955, adoptions and abortions were godless acts that white folks committed. For a single black girl to give her baby away was heinous and almost as bad as her becoming pregnant. Sitting in the court that morning was an act of defiance, for I had overidden many objections to signing adoption papers, especially those of my foster mother. I refused to accept my lot or lie down in the bed that I had made. My pregnancy fulfilled everyone's expectations of me, except my own.

Before I understood what sex was, I was warned that it was an evil inside of me, waiting to pull me into its pulsating pit. My propensity for the dirty act, Mommi said, was even confirmed by the astrological sign I was born under. Her oracles made me, before I fully understood anything about sex, determined to avoid its pitfalls, but as a prepubescent girl, it seemed an amorphous monster that surfaced everywhere. Chalked on the sidewalk, scribbled in textbooks, carved in the school desks, wherever my eyes landed its evil names were waiting. Jumping Double-Dutch in the street in front of my house, I came to understand what society thought of black females, children included, as cars with New Jersey license plates cruised up and down and the drivers beckoned us, waving dollar bills in the air.

Inside our house, sex was such a heavy sin that the word "pregnant" was not allowed. I was unable to differentiate between normal curiosity and my "inherited lowdown ways."

17

I leaned against the white porcelain water tank as if it were a pillow, my two legs rigid as drumsticks piercing the air in order to get a good look at my vagina. Fatty folds of vaginal lips pouted at me in the tiny glass I held between my legs and I was fascinated at the swirls of browns and purples and various textured flesh reflected in it. My fingers carefully separated the two thick dark lips between my thighs and I loved its warm, rising pungent aroma that clung to my fingertips as I stared at the open bulb-shaped mouth with a long thin pulpy tongue that shuddered from the pleasure of my touch. This furtive ritual along with listening to 45 r.p.m. records of Rhythm and Blues gave me pleasure and guilt.

However, the music in the Harlem air in the fifties illuminated my hidden self and gave me the freedom to sing about feelings I did not dare admit having. I was the lead singer of every Rhythm and Blues group singing of longing, loss, and regret. The simple lyrics defined my preordained role, that of a virginal girl waiting for love to happen so that I too could experience heartbreak.

What we couldn't talk about we could sing, and the voice of The Queen of The Blues expressed my hidden, seething, lustful, abstract desires. Dinah's songs, banned in my house and banned from the radio, were ones of comically masked sexual meanings.

As I walked along the street, her sultry voice beckoned to me from every jukebox. I spent stolen moments in the back room of Rainbow's Record Hole where the customers could draw a thick black curtain and listen before buying. Kind Mr. Rainbow would automatically hand me the Queen's 78's and warn me to get out when he had a buying customer. Dinah sang as I danced and swooned to "Fine Fat Daddy," "T.V. Is the Thing This Year" or "Long John Blues." Her voice, swelling and trembling, overflowing with a full-blown exhilaration and a rapturous delight of sex, put flesh on my prurient thoughts.

However, Dinah was not on my mind one June when I was sitting in the hairdresser's booth flinching from a smoking hot comb heading toward my scalp.

"Be still 'for I burn you girl," Miss Paterson, my hairdresser, warned as the shop's rickety door was thrown open.

"Which one of you operators can take The Queen," someone in the doorway purred in spiced velvet tones.

I looked up into a ripe watermelon-red lipsticked mouth and sloe eyes flashing with merriment at the commotion she was causing. Her face was a radiant mixture of dark brown and red hues. She wore a short, white, sleeveless, blouson dress fitted just below her hips with a huge bow that accented her curvaceous behind. Although it was the middle of the day, rhinestones winked and gleamed and glittered on her wrists.

The tiny hairdressing shop with its boarded wooden cubicles and beauty magazine photos of blondes with windswept pageboys took on a new luster as Dinah Washington strode across the floor, her high heels clicking against the wooden slats, her white bow softly bouncing on her behind.

A resident of Harlem, tales of Dinah's salty mouth and numerous marriages were favorite local lore, so after the first wave of excitement subsided, the usual hubbub of the hairdressing shop eased as all ears strained to overhear the conversation between The Queen and her hairdresser.

"Blonde??!" The incredulous voice of Mrs. Spruce, the hairdresser in the booth behind me rose two octaves.

"Yes, girl. I want all my hairs blonde. The Queen is gonna stop traffic on Fifth Avenue!"

"Lordy, Lordy Miss Clawdy, nineteen fourty!" Miss Paterson exclaimed as she burned my right ear with the hot comb in her excitement.

"owwwwwww!" I complained, holding my ear.

"Shhhh," Miss Paterson said, absent-mindedly rubbing Vaseline on my steaming ear while straining to catch the singer's every word.

Her sassy, stinging vibrato rose and fell over intrigued ears as Dinah continued.

"A blonde will make a blind man stiff. I know because husband number four (I don't remember their names, only their numbers) was blind in one eye and couldn't see out the other but his Mister would come to attention anytime a blonde was in the vicinity."

"OuchoooooooW!!!!" I complained as my hairdresser, silently shaking with laughter, accidentally burned my left ear also.

"Hold your ear down, stop fidgeting. You know I got a hot comb in my hand," she replied, trying to sound gruff and absorbed in her work.

Mrs. Spruce's deep scalp massage seemed to loosen Dinah's tongue.

"If you can't beat 'em, join 'em is my motto. All my life I've been told that blondes have more fun. Well darling, I'm the Queen, and no broad is gonna have more fun than me. So unkink my nappy, make it straight and yellow."

Under Mrs. Spruce's expert fingers the singer meandered on.

"This fifth husband I got now tries to reassure me that I got the world's best—" Her voice had sunk into a decent inaudible level but quickly rose again.

"Husband, I say to him now husband, you and I both know that the last one you had is always the best one. Now ain't that right gals? You know it is!"

All the hairdressers and their customers, church matron and street woman, grandmother and schoolgirl hollered out loud because we all understood that Miss Dinah Washington, through her songs and flamboyant style, was telling the world, white, black, and male, that the Queen was one unruly woman. But most females played the game and obeyed the rules, and an unmarried pregnant gal (girls were ladies, gals were sluts) was worse than a boy convicted of a crime. The felon would be encouraged by parents and pastors to repent, serve his time, and start his life anew. No such redemption was urged for an unmarried pregnant gal. When she walked down the street with her belly for all to see, old women peeked and tsked behind the curtains while young ones were glad they were not in her shoes. Merely an object of slander and ridicule, nothing could be done for her. No one wanted to marry her, especially the boy who made her pregnant. And not once in all my growing up years in Harlem did I ever hear the word "abortion" and when I did it was too late. Whatever she did, the pregnant gal would never just get over it. All around me, felled by the S-E-X Demon, abandoned and swollen, gals were just waiting for their time to harvest their shame. When my own time came in 1955, I recalled Fat Helen, her swollen belly, and finally her funeral.

Unyielding to any hue, blank, cold silence, white was always used for the burial of the young so that when Helen and her baby, both in frilly white gowns, lay in a white satin-lined white coffin, the color did not surprise me.

╼

Before the day of her funeral, her body was "on view," the announcement read, at 237 West 117th Street, New York, N.Y. in Apartment 6D. Apartment 6D was on the top floor of a dilapidated tenement, and at the bottom of the stairs, Mommi gazed up an unending flight of stairs and groaned. I wanted to tell her that we had a long, steep, hike in front of us—the elevator hadn't

worked since 1913 A.C. (after colored). I wanted to tell her that
there were thirty-five high steps to each flight. I wanted to tell her
that she should climb the stairs slowly. I didn't want her blood
pressure to rise or her arthritic knee, covered with a piece of flannel soaked in Ben Gay, to ache. I wanted to tell her I was afraid to
go upstairs and look at Helen's dead body. But what was the use? I
was twelve years old and we hadn't had a civil conversation in
years.

As we started the long climb she groaned and panted and
began a familiar litany. I-guess-this-proves-that-I-was-right about
Helen all along.

*Here you go. I know what's coming. Every bad thing that happens
in the world it is as if I had done it.*

You'll be following in her footsteps if I don't keep my eye on
you.

At least if I was dead I wouldn't have to hear this.

Climbing the stairs behind her I fought the urge to stick my
fingers in my ears.

She stood still, holding on to the bannister, breathing heavily
and glaring at me. She saw my gap tooth, my huge behind, my
sensuality, and my independence. What she saw in me was my
natural rebelliousness, a refusal to be broken down by her will like
everyone else around her. And what she saw reminded her of May
Anna. I stared back. I noticed the quickening gray strands in her
thinning hair, her woolen overcoat she had worn forever. I sensed
her anger at growing old and having nothing after decades of hard
work, her frustration at being unable to move from Harlem, her
fear of dangers on the streets that awaited young girls. I just hated
it that she was so furious with me all the time.

Mommi fished for something in her pocketbook, and finding a
clipping from the *Daily Mirror,* pressed it into my hand. "See what
is happening just up the street from us in the next block a couple of
houses from us, this could be you if I weren't as decent as I am.
Read it!" she ordered. I remember that in that dim, malodorous

hallway, on my way up six steep flights of rickety, rotting stairs to view Helen's dead body, I kept a long stream of schoolchildren and their parents waiting as I stood still and read:

NEIGHBORS MOURN GIRL WHO NEVER HAD A CHANCE

On 327 West 120th Street youngest children play on the sidewalks or cling to their mothers on the front stoops and everyone seems to linger outside most of the time waiting for the heat to snap.

The neighbors on Ebony's block say that they noticed something "going on" with the child. Time and again, they saw her running in tears from the building, huddling in doorways with men probably twice her age. She was just past her 13th birthday, and the neighbors said that it was not uncommon for her to dash home at nearly any hour of the night or not show up at all. Ebony's body was found two weeks ago burning beneath a highway overpass in the Bronx. "She was the saddest thing you ever saw," said the neighbors. "She never had a chance. She never slept on a bed with sheets, always on a bare mattress and fed Kool-Aid."

"What does this have to do with me?" I yelled, crumbling the clipping in my hand. But she didn't even hear me, for she began huffing and puffing up the stairs again. "I am tired of being every juvenile delinquent you read about in the *Daily Mirror*!" I said to her ascending back.

Mommi was scared. So was I. Maybe the words she was really saying to me were "I love you and I only want to protect you from these dangerous Harlem streets." Maybe. Maybe, I thought, there was some wicked alchemy, some evil magic, that distorted what she meant to be words of love and concern and made them sound like Mark my words, if it weren't for me you would be just like the rest of the trashy riffraff in Harlem. Mark my words.

On the fifth flight of stairs, Sister Rosetta Tharpe's shivering, husky alto accompanied by a pealing organ and gloomy chimes floated down from an open Victrola. Her trembling moans were sanctified and lustful. In her voice there was no difference between religious fervor and sexual ecstasy.

Looks a loving father

Down on every ev-e-ry chile

Incense pinched my nose as we neared the top floor. Finally at the sixth floor we faced an open apartment door, and a coffin. Incense and roses clogged the air.

Mommi and I fall into the line of mourners snaking slowly toward the coffin.

They are weak

It is Assembly Day and all the girls wear starched white middy blouses with a scratchy sailor collar and a pleated blue skirt. All the boys wear white shirts and ties. Red ties for eighth grade, blue for the ninth.

And He is stroooong.

Helen's white shroud comes into my line of sight. Do dead girls wear brassieres? Is it white also? What shade of white? Eggshell? Ivory?

God bless ev-e-ry chile

Left, right, left, right. One foot in front of the other. Closer and closer Helen's corpse looms before my eyes.

"This is Helen who just returned from down South," said Miss Hamblin our ninth grade teacher. Standing in front of us was Fat Helen, now an embarrassed, curvaceous girl, not the chubby bodacious ringleader, tormentor of my childhood, the friend-enemy, who once lived underneath me. Now she was a timid, moon-face ripe girl who under the glare of our stares humped her shoulders over a few inches but still could not hide her bulging breasts.

Helen and her mother had left 120th Street to take care of her grandmother in Virginia. Miss Hamblin, who held anything she took from us between her second and third finger with as little handling as

*possible, was so flustered by the uproar Helen's sweater was causing,
she accidentally touched Helen as she pointed out her desk.*

*She was older than the rest of us but everyone knew that the New
York City Board of Education automatically put black kids from the
South a grade behind when they came to New York. I was glad. I had
finally caught up with her. But not physically. There stood Helen, her
full breasts taunting my flat chest. On her sweater, the outline of her
brassiere mocked my cotton ribbed undershirt.*

Mommi and I shuffled onward ever moving closely to the
body. O Helen.

> Touch! I said Touch Not
> A single hair on they head

Slowly, slowly creeping toward her. Left foot and then the right.

> For the Wee Ones are weak
> And My Father soooooooooStrong,
> Ahhhhhhmmmmmmmmmm!

The needle scratches against the vinyl record with a screeching
sound before the music ends. The small, crowded room buzzes
with a din of grief as we crawl forward. As we draw close, I know
that the sight of my friend in a casket in the middle of the room
where we used to play will haunt me forever. Involuntarily, I grab
Mommi's hand. She lets me. I close my eyes.

*At long last you and I were girlfriends. This room was our secret away
from our warring guardians, away from the ceaseless nagging, accusations, and prohibitions. A huge four-poster bed used to be in the center
of the room in the very spot where you are now laying in your casket.*

Remember how we used to leaf through Movie Star, *claiming John
Derek and Farley Granger as ours?*

Then slowly, against my will, my eyes open.

Madonna and child in a gleaming white satin, whose sheen
makes their dead faces seem all the more dull and ashen. Their
matching white lace gowns are edged in white rosebuds.

I can't stay long.

So. What shall we do.

I know. Wanna see my new Popeye comic?

Ha ha, look. Popeye's dick grows bigger as he eats his spinach.

Ohhh, it just ran off the page.

I know. Let's write love letters to each other and pretend we are girlfriend and boyfriend.

No. I gotta better thing. Let's sing "Ikey and Mikey."

Okay.

Ikey and Mikey
Were playing in a ditch
Ikey called Mikey
A dirty son of a
Bring down your chirren
And let them play with sticks
When they get older
Let them play with
Dickey had a baby
His name was Tiny Tim
He put him in a piss-pot
Taught him how to swim
He swam to the bottom
He swam to the top
And when he got older
He learned to play with
Cocktails and gingerale
Ten cents a glass
And if you don't like it
I'll stick it up your
Ask me no questions
I'll tell you no lie
Else you'll get hit
With a bag of shit
And that's the reason why!

Hahahahahahahahahaha
Let's do that again.

We loved maleness but we hated boys. They were annoying, teasing, audacious creatures with a bomb in their pants. Gazing down at her, I apologized to Helen for turning away from her when she needed a friend more than ever. But school was my only sanctuary and between Miss Hamblin and the other kids it was just too heavy being her friend.

On the day you vomited your school lunch of tomato soup and pea-nut butter sandwich and when some of it splashed on fastidious Miss Hamblin she almost fainted. When Miss Hamblin returned after a week of sick leave you were still throwing up but you never missed a day of school. Soon your nausea ceased and things in the classroom re-turned to normal except Miss Hamblin refused to call on you.

Cradled in dead Helen's arms is her crushed baby. Is it a boy?

Miss Hamblin pretended to be oblivious to the hum of uproar your pregnancy caused in our classroom. You were the first in class every morning. You took a seat in the back and left immediately by the rear dooor at the first ring of three o'clock.

Or a girl?

Helen, you pretended not to notice, not to care when I went along with everyone else and teased you about your heavy bulky sweaters in warm weather and your sitting with your arms folded across your stomach, always grabbing your elbows as if to hug yourself.

Helen, I pretended not to notice how you always sat with your face toward the window.

I lifted my head and gazed around the room at the grieving mothers and fathers, teachers, boys and girls. Now, dead and no longer a threat, everyone was looking at Helen. She was more vis-ible now than she ever was when she was alive.

"O GOD! " A voice crackled across the room.

Parents kept us away from you, saying you were just a "bad girl," and refused to say anything else.

"O GOD! O GOD!" repeated the voice.

You pretended you were just getting heavier and wore tighter gir-dles and looser blouses.

"GOD?" questioned the voice.

Helen, even you pretended you were invisible.

"*PLEASE GOD*" begged the voice.

As your belly billowed you became more invisible.

"PLEASE GOD!" begged the voice." DEAR GOD," prayed the voice. "GOD!"

My voice sounded in my ears, a disembodied echo. From my roots, swelling and gathering force, a tidal wave of anger, rushing forth from my every corner, came crashing through my mouth, curses disguised as a mourner's cry. I sobbed in words that sounded like OGOD! OGOD! OGOD! But I was really saying, "GOD-DAMN! GODDAMN! ALL OF YOU HERE! Who cared about her, Helen had nobody, not even me." Ostensibly I stumbled and had to grab Helen's coffin with both hands but I was really trying to kick it and smash it,. To those looking on it must have appeared that I raised my hands in grief but I really wanted to slap some sense in Helen's dead face until she became alive again. My machine-gun sobs were not grief for the dead but anger at the living. They were howls of fury, curses masked as lamentations.

"Let's go," said Mommi softly, gently urging me to take a step forward. "We have to pay our respects to Mrs. Field and make room for others."

As I moved away from dead Helen I thought about those days not so long ago when she and I tapped coded messages on painted radiators and sizzling aluminum-painted pipes.

Now Mrs. Field, her face bathed in candlelight, slowly moved her thick, broken, parched, tear-swollen lips as Mommi offered her a box of fried chicken and a homemade pound cake wrapped in wax paper. "Thank you, God bless you for coming."

18

Rose had different problems. "I will not get married," she screamed at her mother one day. The princess of the house, she was seven years older and I envied her legitimate blood, her right-handedness, her petite frame, her dark, satiny skin, and her face, a replica of Mrs. Feral's with full wide lips, high cheekbones, and intense brown eyes. Every morning I watched as she dressed in the uniform she wore downtown to Cathedral High School—a navy blue beret she tilted to one side, an austere, pleated jumper and white blouse, and thick orangey cotton stockings and blue Oxford shoes that on Rose's skinny legs managed to appear sexy.

She was a princess with an aura of enchantment. One moment Rose was among us, the next moment she was gone. Then, faint at first, then slowly growing in sound, tempo, and passion, her piano playing would wash over us. Whether a simple, plaintive melody or a tumultuous dramatic outpouring of notes, her music suspended and bewitched us. Docile and soft-spoken, Rose was transformed at her piano, her fingers flying over the keys weaving fiery arpeggios or lush harmonies. Rose spent hours at the ebony grand piano that competed for space with a couch and two arm-chairs whose ample plastic covers looked like construction-site tarpaulin.

She entered the room reverently, softly closed the curtained

French doors. Then, before she opened it, Rose would stand before the closed piano, her head bowed. Next, Rose would sit on the piano bench, her back in a straight line, her fingers arched and suspended in midair before they descended upon the keys.

When Rose entered Cathedral High School instead of Harlem's notorious Wadleigh High, Mrs. Feral mysteriously disappeared on Saturday mornings. She did not return to us until very late. Unknown to us at the time—she had cleaned house, scrubbed floors, washed clothes, and cooked all day for a family on Park Avenue.

One rainy Saturday, Rose was left alone to watch over me, and suddenly we were lords and masters of the apartment. She went to a small wooden cabinet that was hidden in the bottom of a closet in her bedroom. Bending down, she opened it and exposed a jug with an imperial crown engraved on its glass neck. Putting the jug in the middle of the floor, Rose knelt before it as she unscrewed its cap. "It's the same wine they use for communion," she said piously, "and I feel religious." She placed her wine-red lipsticked lips around the bottle, tilted the jug, and thirstily sucked up the red liquid. "My turn," I yelled. "Just a little bit," she warned as I drank. I was surprised at its taste. The wine did not taste like something that was ruby red. Instead it tasted purplish, heavy and cloying, almost bitter in its sweetishness.

"Let's dance," Rose yelled, and we dashed to the parlor and quickly rolled back the rug. I wound up our RCA Victrola while Rose hurriedly searched through a pile of 45 r.p.m. records. Soon the Duke of Iron's hit song "Stone Cold Dead In De Market Place" followed by Lord Invader's "Out De Fire" rang in the room, and Rose grabbed me around my waist and guided me from one end of the parlor to the other as we twisted our hips from side to side in a wild and erotic calypso.

"We have to hurry cause Mommi might be home soon," Rose cautioned as she changed the music to "Dutch Kitchen Bounce" by Arnett Cobb.

"We're in the *Daily News* Harvest Moon Ball Contest. We are Jitterbug Queens and our pictures are gonna be in the centerfold," said Rose as we started doing the Lindy Hop. She pulled me through her legs and swung me in a circle, lifting me off the floor. "Now I'm going to dip you," she warned as she bent me backward, making my head touch the floor and my eyes parallel to the ceiling. I fell flat on my back and Rose fell on top of me laughing and said, "Oh, Gin-gin, you are just a left-handed girl with two left feet."

We grew up as sisters with bonds stronger than blood, but now unhappy Rose had her own troubles. Crying with the beasts of inchoate rage hovering around her head, she repeated, "I will not get married, and you can't make me!"

"Act like a girl of your class. I'm just thinking of our reputation," Mrs. Feral called running after her. "Stop acting . . . like," she said, looking at me, "someone else's child."

"You rot inside because of what people might say," Rose sniffled.

"Don't be disrespectful. I run a decent house. Everyone knows what a respectable family we are. You don't come off the streets. You have a family name to live up to. Act like my daughter, be true to your blood. Why can't you do this one thing that I ask?"

19

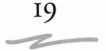

The pilfered port wine on that rainy Saturday afternoon was brought up in a routine miscellaneous whipping I received on Sunday, appropriately given on the Lord's day for she intended to beat the devil out of me. When the metal connector of her iron cord struck the base of my spine and paralyzed me for a second, Rose begged Mommi to stop.

Too sore to sleep, I lay awake late that night. Quickly I closed my eyes as I heard the pitter-patter of her slippers toward my room. I could feel her come into the kitchen and turn on the light. I could feel the glow of the sudden brightness as it shone under the door along the floor of my room and was petrified as her soft slippers whispered toward my bed. She looked down where I pretended to sleep and closed her eyes. When she bent down low close to my face, her tears were flowing and running toward her mouth. She flicked her tongue in and out as if to taste them before they fell on my face. Abruptly she left my room and I wiped my eyes, refusing to let my own tears run down my cheek and mix with hers. I was too furious to even wonder what her tearful nocturnal visit to my bed could mean. Whatever it was, I didn't care.

On Monday, Mommi, Teddie, and I sit in the waiting room of the Sheltering Arms Children's Service building on 29th Street and Lexington Avenue, waiting for my annual physical by the hoary Dr. Regan. I shift my weight carefully to avoid putting painful pressure on my behind. But in spite of my caution, the expected jolt of pain flashes from the base of my spine as I reach for the newspaper on the table in front of me. After the throbbing pain subsides I look at Mrs. Feral who is sitting beside me. Sitting upright and rigid, her every cell at attention, her plump hands fold and unfold in her lap, her burnished brown skin firm, glowing. She quickly glances at me and looks away. I wish I could tell someone. What would happen to her if I said something? Bet she's afraid I'll tell them. I should tell them. That will fix her, I muse. I see her fidgeting hands. I know that she is nervous every time she has to bring us to these annual inspections; that she regards them as a test to see how she is doing her job; a test she wants to pass. After all, we are foster children worth so many dollars and she doesn't want to be fired. Mommi makes a flash inspection of Teddie and me to see if we are still clean and then, running her hands through her graying hair, quickly checks her own appearance to make sure the silver buttons that run down the front of her blue and white polka dot dress have not popped open.

"Pow, bip, bam," prattles Teddie on the floor as she whips her doll.

Next to her, on his knees, a little boy with a cap on and woolen stockings and knickers is slowly building a tower of blocks, determined to defy gravity.

Sheltering Arms Children's Service on New York's fashionable East Side had once been the private residence of a very wealthly family. I loved climbing the short flight of stone steps and opening its mahogany and brass filigree main door. In spite of its conversion to its present use, many of the ornately decorated archways and curving staircases had been preserved.

With only three floors, I wonder what is on the other floors. I have been visiting the building for annual checkups and selection of used clothes and have never been on any floor but this one, which has been converted into offices, examining rooms, and playrooms. Now the room is filled with foster mothers and older foster children who, like me, are bored and irritable, sitting on sticky vinyl couches waiting for a turn to see Dr. Regan while the younger ones play with with toys.

As I turn the rectangular pages of the *New York Times,* I long for the comics in the *Daily News* and wonder what Gravel Gertie and Pear Shape and B.O. Plenty in Dick Tracy are doing today.

"I told you to use your right hand in public," hisses Mommi as my left hand bumps against her arm as I turn another page.

"Bad dolly POW bad Girlie, BAM! I'll kick your hips in. WHAM." In Teddie's left hand is a dirty, battered, button-eyed, florid rag doll, a blood rosebud mouth smeared across her face and orange yarn tightly knotted to its pinkish scalp. In Teddie's right hand is an imaginary strap with which she pounds the backside of the unfortunate toy.

"Pow pow pow pow pow!" she continues

I swear I see tears creep out of the doll's button eyes.

"No Ow, I'm bleeding now I won't do it anymore pleasepleaseplease Owwwww I'm bleeding.I won't do it anymore," Teddie begs in a falsetto. Is she mocking me on the sly? When the doctor finally calls us I follow Mommi into the examining room, staring at the imprint of her corset on her dress.

"Sure and is this the same wee mite with the misery in her lungs, the wee baby that we thought would not make it through the night, Mrs. Feral?" greets the old doctor. His Irish tongue has the same cadences of the West Indian lilt I am used to hearing.

"If I had known that she would turn out to be my crown of thorns, my cross, I would have never—"

"Sure it is a worrying age. But you're doing God's work, you are."

"With God's help," says Mommi as she piously rolls her eyes heavenward. "I believe God sends us evil, he also sends with it the weapon to conquer it."

Trying to avoid the pain I gingerly begin my ascent up to the high examination table. "Owwwwww!" I yelp as I jump involuntarily and cautiously sit down leaning on the outer ridge of my right behind to carefully avoid the spot where sparks of pain shoot in the bottom of my buttocks.

"It hurts there?" asked Dr. Regan incredulously pointing to the base of my spine. I shrink from his probing fingers.

"Let the doctor examine you," commands Mommi.

"It hurts there?" he repeats. "How did you get a sore coccyx?"

He is wrinkled and solemn, his eyes pale blue behind thick, rimless glasses.

I concentrate on the strange word and mentally add it to my collection. The room is small and the grey walls, except for the NAACP Alfred Schweitzer Missionary Award are bare. On a cluttered desk is a faded photograph of young Dr. Regan with black hair in a tent in an African outpost posing with smiling naked black children.

"How in heaven's name did ye get a sore coccyx?" the old doctor repeats.

"Nothing," I mumble. Tell him, I said to myself, but I remain quiet.

"She got a whipping. Just this past Saturday. That's how," replies Mommi without hesitation. "A good hard old-fashioned whipping. Lord, how this girl provokes me so."

I want to disappear into the naked walls. Instead I just stare at her defiantly.

"You see how she stares at me in that rude tone of voice," Mommi appeals to the doctor. "She likes beatings."

As he places his cold stethoscope around my neck I am glad

that I only have to open my blouse down the front. I don't want him to see the old marks, ugly scars and the long red welts crisscrossed on my back.

His white hair shines with a silvery sparkle as he leans his head close to me, tapping my chest, cautioning, "Got the divil in ye now, is that so? Young lady, ye would fare better if ye behave yourself, lass."

I hang my head.

Mommi's hands are folded quietly in her lap as the old doctor touches the bottom of my spine again as if to see if I am faking.

"OOwwOoo," I wail angrily.

"A hooligan is she now," he half inquires half states, with an amused disinterest.

"Foolishness is bound in the heart of a child. Only the rod of correction shall take it away," Mommi intones, while I furiously think how I hate the goddamn Bible and furthermore, I'm not too happy about God these days.

"Mother, has she had her period yet?" asks the doctor, gazing through me.

"Just this spring."

"Fast blooms, these gals."

"Fast in body and mind," sighs Mommi wearily, "but I keep a careful watch."

Yes she does. And when she's not watching, Aunt Syl is.

"Fit as a fiddle," pronounces the doctor as he washes his hands.

"Doctor, can you give her something to help her use her right hand? Just like the sinful people of Ninevah she uses her left hand."

"Ho, ho, ha, ha," chuckled Dr. Regan as he looked at me. "Ninevah, that wicked city that God sent Jonah to save? She's not like them, Mrs. Feral. You do know good from evil now, don't you child?"

"Bible say the devil holds his sword in his left hand, you know," reminds Mommi.

"Too late now. She should have been broken earlier. "

"I tried. Stubborn."

"Maybe it's inherited."

"That figures, " sighed Mommi resignedly. "What about her bed wetting, then?"

"Still bed wetting are ye now, young lass?"

A live coal of shame burned my throat.

"Mother, have you tried boiled pumpkin seeds?"

"Flaxseed tea, fish-eye broth, green soursop, crush sapodilla, nightshade, vervain, boiled water, sea water, no water."

"No luck?"

"She pee and more pee. Maybe I should tie a tin can around her leg like they do 'em back home and when the pee-bed walked down the streets the whole parish sings

red red pee the bed
stew in pee until you dead."

"Maybe she'll grow out of it," offered Dr. Regan

"I hope she does before she pee up my sheets. My back break from leaning over the tub, and my knuckles wear out on the scrub board every day washing out her pee sheets."

"Got a rubber sheet?"

"Got two of them I do. Her pee goes right through the rubber. I'm telling you. I believe she pees in the bed on purpose."

"Take a course of coal powder and aloes. Half a dose of coal powder, add 3 tablespoons of aloe, mix a little water once per 9 days. Give her an enema. Relax for one or two weeks. Repeat routine." Dr. Regan continues washing his hands and then without looking at me he says, "Young lady, stop worrying your foster mother. Thank your lucky stars you are receiving a nice Christian upbringing in a fine foster home. Behave yourself and see you next year."

20

The courtroom clock struck eleven A.M. The sound was an indifferent golden chime, unmindful of the doom it presaged. Mrs. Walling stretched out her arms toward me. "Let me hold Kelvin a while so you can get some rest." Although I had been dealing with social workers all my life, Mrs. Georgia Wallings was only the second one whose conversations did not sound like a textbook. She was so empathetic, the girls at Inwood House said, because she had given up a child up for adoption when she was young. How else could she be so understanding, so warm and loving?

She was indeed a rarity. She lived in the Village, was divorced and was very beautiful with thick brown hair, brown eyes, and a mole right at the tip of her full red lips. The workers I had grown up with in the forties and early fifties came from Schools of Social Work in places like Atlanta, Cleveland, Missouri, and Wisconsin. These women (there were never any men) wore tweed suits, brown Oxford shoes with laces, carried briefcases. Groping in the darkness of their prejudices they peered at us and spoke to us oddly, incapable of normal human communication. Gee whiz, one exclaimed as she was concluding her home visit. This has been informative. Most delightful. It is the first time I've sat down and chatted with a Negro. New to New York, they were resentful of their uptown assignments, frightened and ill at ease when they came to our house. Those timid white girls from the Middle West were no match for the Harlem termagant, and all were silent before Mommi's formidable, cold brown eyes, dominating personality, and strong will. That is, all except one.

21

"Read this and pass it on," said the young woman as she thrust a pamphlet from the War Resistors League into Mommi's hand.

THE ARMS RACE

Is a clear sign of the direction and spirit of our age.

Relations between people are corrupted by distorted images.

Spiritual destitution is rampant and manifested in VIOLENCE.

WE MUST ALL DISARM NOW!

"Communist," Mommi mumbled under her breath as she tossed the paper into the garbage. I made a note to rescue it from the trash as I tried to conceal my pleasure.

"How's the fastest reader in the East?" she greeted me as she entered our apartment. "How many books this month?"

No matter how many books I told her, Miss Mullens would ask, feigning disappointment, "is that all?" Then she would lean close to me and whisper "ailanthus" or some other unfamiliar word, daring me to know it in time for her next visit. Dressed in bright, seamless shifts, sandals, and black stockings, in our living room she interrupted Mommi's litany of complaints about me with a "Try psychology," "I don't believe in violence."

"I believe in the old-fashioned way where a hard head makes a soft behind and those who don't hear, feel," said Mommi enraged.

"Disarmament starts in the home. Why is it wrong to beat your wife but not your children? Would you beat your dog?"

"I don't have a dog," replied Mommi.

"And if you had one I bet you're too kind to beat it," answered Miss Mullens sweetly.

Twice a year I was forced to trek to Thomfordes Ice Cream Parlor with my social worker, where she routinely probed for any problems I might be having. Holding my brown hand with one hand and her briefcase in the other, I always had to scurry beside an apprehensive white woman, feeling very nervous about her whiteness, while her briefcase and walking shoes broadcast to everyone on the street that I was a child welfare case and she was my worker.

But today with Miss Mullens it is different. She puts her arms around my shoulders as we stroll down 125th Street taking in the sights. We window shop and suck on the sugar cane bought from a truck farmer on Seventh Avenue. Even though she is the best social worker I ever had, I am a veteran of these interrogations. I know better than to reveal anything at these routine ice-cream inquisitions, for after all, she is still white and I am no traitor.

As soon as we enter Thomfordes Ice Cream Parlor we are enclosed in a rainbow of aromas. Is it chocolate? Nutmeg? Banana? Cinnamon? It is everything delicious to eat in that store commingling into one indescribably sweet aroma.

Excitement buzzes in the air. Folks are smiling and animated because they know something delicious is about to happen. Straining to sit still while waiting for my ice cream, I secretly swing my legs and tap my feet, humming happily under my breath.

Miss Mullens and I sit in the high-backed wooden booths that resemble church pews. The silver ice-cream dishes and long-handled ice-cream spoons seem appropriate sacramental articles for this rite. The waitresses look like sexy sancitifed church saints, with their white caps and shoes, dark skins gleaming against pale uniforms. As they serve their customers, fragrances of vanilla, almond, and cinnamon cling to them, and their black-raspberry lips indiscriminately call us "sugar," "baby," and "darlin," in voices thick with honey. I dream about the coming taste of the dark gooey hot fudge being prepared just for me, I can't wait to see the dark chocolate sliding on a bed of creamy, frosty vanilla.

Miss Mullens grabs my hands and pleads, "I know there must be some things you want to tell me," and looks deep into my eyes.

As I painstakingly suck the syrup off of each wedge of walnut lodged in my mouth I think of See No Evil, Hear No Evil, and Speak No Evil, the three brass monkeys on the bookcase that Mommi shows me each time a worker comes to escort me to Thomfordes.

"No, nothing," I mumble, lost in a haze of whip cream. Previously, I was always on guard not to reveal anything. But today, with Miss Mullens and the lightness of the whipped cream combined with the sweet, thick, gooey fudge sticking to the roof of my mouth, I am intoxicated and my tongue becomes unhinged.

"You know what I hate?" I asked suddenly as I put my tongue through the hole in a maraschino cherry and split its juicy red skin. "The space between my teeth. Lie-gaps she call them. Everything I say is either lies or back-talk. Words are my only defense. Books are my only escape but she calls me a bookworm and says they give me rude ideas. Do you know anything about my real mother? I'm used to the whippings now but can't you stop her from calling May Anna a worthless slut who dropped her load, me, and ran?"

When I see the look on her face I know I have talked too much, gone too far. The sweetness of my ice cream has turned flat. My bananas are soggy, lumpen mush.

Miss Mullens leans over. Her voice trembles as she lays her hand on top of mine. "I thought so. It's time someone wrote a truthful report on her."

"No!" I scream.

"Don't worry. I won't say you said a thing."

"No! No!"

"Don't be afraid."

"No. No," I am shaking and crying.

"Mrs. Feral's taken care of babies for the city since 1929, but she's never had a child your age. Their mothers have always taken them back before she can do them any real harm. Even Teddie has Muriel to protect her."

I feel so ashamed. "Where is my mother? Where is May Anna? Can you tell me?"

"No, I can't, but suppose," says Miss Mullens, "I can find a nice pacifist home for you where no one believed in beatings?"

"I'd stay right where I am," I answer, pulling my hand away from hers.

"Why?" asks Miss Mullens as she again reaches for my hand.

"Because, just because." My throat aches with tears.

"Suppose," she continues burying my hands in hers, "I find you a nice foster mother and father that did not believe in beatings?"

I feel nauseous.

"Suppose I know a young, progressive, pacifist couple, in the peace movement, that wants to share their home with a child like you. All you—"

"No, no. You can't make me go. I won't," I scream.

"Don't be afraid. She won't know you said anything. I promise."

"No!"

"But why not, after all you've just told me?" asks Miss Mullens incredulously.

"No!"

"Why?"

"Because I owe her. She's the one that's been feeding and clothing me all these years," I say echoing Mommi's words, trying hard not to cry.

"The city clothes and feeds you. Not Mrs. Feral," Miss Mullens whispers, almost to herself as she quietly withdraws her hands from mine.

"But it's not enough and she has to spend her own money."

"Is that what she tells you? It's not true."

"So what? She's still my mother and I don't want to go to live with strangers," I cry as I push away my ice cream.

I never breathe a word to anyone about our conversation but still it is the last time I ever see Miss Mullens. I am glad. Somehow, I didn't want to see her anymore.

22

"I'm Miss LeNoire, your new social worker," the tall woman greets us in 1950. She has long black glossy hair, with a rosy skin and is the first black social worker we have ever seen.

"LeNoire," gushes Mommi. "You wouldn't at all be related to Judge Theophilus LeNoire in Philadelphia?"

"You know my family?"

"Only through the society columns. Then your uncle is Reverend Sebastian LeNoire, pastor of St. Xavier in Philadelphia?"

"I admit it. I'm a judge's daughter and a minister's niece," the tall woman slyly bragged.

"You look just like your pictures in the *Amsterdam*," complimented Mommi.

"Oh, those awful photos," complained the tall woman, tossing her shiny black curls.

"You know that society columnist in the *Amsterdam News?*"

"Oh her, Gerri Major . . ."

"Yes, I always see your picture in her column. I study the society columns."

"She's a friend of the family."

Mommi is titillated. "After all these years in these agency, they have finally sent me a worker who is someone of my own ilk."

"Oh yes," agrees Miss LeNoire. "When will they learn that we are not all the same?"

"Some of those other workers were one half step above white trash, thinking they can march into Harlem and tell me how to raise children."

"I know you set them straight."

"I sure do. I let them know, we don't let our children run all over them the way they do."

"That's right, Mrs. Feral, we sure don't."

"Oh yes, there's no problem in this house cause I know the way to an unruly child's mind is through her behind."

"Oh, ha ha ha ha, Mrs. Feral, you're a poet."

"Don't I know it," Mommi agrees. In the middle of laughing Miss LeNoire notices Teddie and me for the first time.

"Theodora Miriam Louis. What big pretty eyes you have," she coos, bending down besides Teddie. "But why whip dolly like that?"

"She has to get her whipping so she'll be good, "answered Teddie softly.

"Ohhh, are you bad too? Do you get whippings?"

"No," said Teddie, looking at me. "Not me."

"That's a good girl," replied the new social worker. Turning to speak to me for the first time, her dark eyes are now distant, hard, judge and jury.

"Nice to meet you. I've heard a lot about you."

Flustered, suddenly embarrased, feeling shy and awkward, without thinking I extended my wrong hand to her as she attempted to shake my hand.

"You mean you are unruly enough to shake with your left hand," Mommi says, her dark eyes dangerous.

"She's not being unruly, Mrs. Feral," replies the new social worker as I stand with my hands now glued to my side, too embarrassed, ashamed, and angry to reach for her hand.

"Oh no, she's not being unruly," Miss LeNoire smiles at me, "because unruly foster girls go to the orphanage where they wouldn't have their own room, and their own bed, like she does."

"Do they have their own iron-cord whipping almost every day?" I wonder.

As if reading my mind, Miss LeNoire continues, "And there is corporal punishment. So you aren't being unruly now, are you?"

"No ma'm," I answer, extending my right hand to the new, pretty, tall, black social worker, hating her almost as much as I hate Mrs. Feral.

They sip highballs of scotch and soda and eat dainty ribbon sandwiches from ivory-colored, silver-ringed china dishes. Enchanted by this creamy daughter of Philidelphia society, Mommi always wears her good dress and powders her nose in anticipation of her visits. I pretend to read in my room as I eavesdrop on their conversations.

"I may live in Harlem but I'm not of Harlem. Back in Bermuda we had white folks doing our laundry!"

The two women find comfort in one another. Miss LeNoire feeds Mommi various tidbits about her family, especially her mother, a well-known club woman.

"I've got to make a big splash here in New York. You know the pressure of the expectation of a family who has a paragraph in 'Negro High Society in the United States.'"

And when Miss LeNoire and Mommi had their photos published in the *Amsterdam* at Sheltering Arms Dinner for Foster Parents they were ecstatic.

"It's in the *Amsterdam!*"

"Ohhhhh Lemme seeee!"

"Who's that standing behind us. See her face peeking out?"

"That's the Borough President's wife."

"Oh, Hulan Jack? I'm in the same photo with both of them?"

"Mmmm."

"Harlem woman and Judge's Daughter at Foster Care Agency Banquet at Hotel Theresa."

"Wait till the folks back in Philly see this!"

"Wait till folks around here see it."

"It's not bad as far as newspaper photos go. Mmmmm, these sandwiches are delish. What are they?"

"Potted meat and tuna."

"Delish. I wish I had worn something else to the affair."

"Let me freshen your glass. See how dark I look."

"Least you look halfway decent with your gloves and hat. I didn't wear any."

"See, you got a nice smile. See, me frowning to beat the band?"

"One cube, one ice cube is enough. You look alright to me."

"I always come out looking like this. See, you're smiling, see how you're smiling with your hands on my shoulders and see, Hulan Jack is smiling and his wife is so beautiful and see me looking like a headache about to happen!"

"No you don't I—"

"Look, see, my face looking like a peach pit!"

"Okay then. Why didn't you smile?"

"Never! I got mirrors, I know how I look. . . . Folks think I'm getting rich being a foster mother. I don't even have enough money to get my mouth fixed."

"Still, you look just fine. What you put in these highballs? Delish."

"Me, look fine? Don't lie. A touch of bitters."

"Angostura bitters?"

"Your hair looks lovely in this photo."

"Oh, my hair. I got my looks from my father the judge. Wait till he sees this picture."

"My papa dead back in Bermuda."

"Really? These cashews are delish. What happened to him?"

"Bought his own land. Built his own house. Had stables and a groom man. Private pew in the parish church. White folks did our laundry."

"So what happened to him?"

"He swim like a fish but we were told he drowned."

"I don't understand."

"Girl, put two and two. You can add, can't you?"

"Oh, I see. Because of things like that. My mother's uncle moved his house from South Carolina to Virgina."

"Do tell? A whole house?"

"It's true. Cellar and all."

"I believe it."

"They say he died trying to figure how to move it to Canada, or France. Now, we may have roots in the South but if there were ever any slaves in our family, I don't know anything about them."

"I know what you mean. We ourselves were always high class, even now, without money."

"I did hear some talk about our being descendants of an American President though."

"Seems to me I hear every light-skin American lay the same claim."

"Ain't it the truth. Except it's true in our case."

"You don't say. Well, of course, we don't put much stock in the ole tale that our family roots go back to William the Conqueror. English aristocracy on my mother's side. Talk has it that my grandmother was impregnated by Sir Eric Cootie—the Lieutnant Governor of Bermuda."

"Was your grandmother a slave?"

"We never used the word. She was in service."

"Oh. Oh, this paté is simply delish."

"I hate it when they lump all colored people together."

"So do I."

"Syl and I do not get along with colored Americans."

"Why, pray tell?"

"Cause we are decent and hard working, we want to get someplace and we stick together. All they want to do is collect welfare and rabblerouse. Most of them are riffraff."

"I see. It was a grand affair. The banquet and the award. Wasn't it?"

"Imagine. A banquet at the elegant Hotel Theresa."

"Plush and grand I'd say."

"Wasn't the cuisine simply delish?"

"I hardly knew which fork to use."

"Crepe suzettes."

"Mussels ravigote."

"Vichyssoise."

"Coq au vin."

"Richelin torte."

"Chateau De Estephe Vintage 1900."

"Makes me think about when Syl and I and Percival first arrived. Who would have guessed that I would ever dine at the Hotel Theresa?"

"You always lived with your sister and husband together?"

"Always. Why shouldn't we. We bred in the same womb and suckle at the same breast. No man is gonna separate us."

"I thought my family was clannish but I think you West Indians got us beat."

"Bermuda is in the Atlantic, not the Carribean . . . We not West Indians."

"Well, you sound like one."

"That's a British accent. We are British subjects."

"Why did you leave Bermuda?"

There was a long silence.

"When the three of us got to this country we had five dollars between us and we got here just in time to greet the Depression."

"How did you make it?"

"By pulling together. I remember the first day we came out the subway station at 125th Street. We had never seen so many smartly dressed colored people. Brutish folks shoved us out the way while others nodded and tipped their hats. Rabble-rousers were on the corner shouting at the top of their lungs about Marcus Garvey."

"They still there."

"Shoot. I remember one, a redbone black American with a slight limp who waved and shouted hoarsely, said his lungs was gassed in the War and called himself Manman, Knight in the Distinguished Order of Ethiopia. That same day, we saw our first Harlem funeral for a big-time colored."

"Ohh, tell me. What was it like?"

"A band played When The Saints Go Marching In. A group of uniformed lodge members following and then automobiles with piles of roses, a tower of red ones, four feet wide and eight feet high with white satin ribbons fluttering to the top, creeping down Seventh Avenue."

"Harlem loves weddings and funerals don't they?"

"Without saying a word to each other, Syl and I followed the funeral procession to 137th Street to Mother Zion. Folks were leaning out of windows. Lenox and Seventh Avenues were thronged. We just stood looking. We learned that it was the funeral of a colored actress who had gone to Europe, became a star, and returned to America and died at the age of thirty-one."

"Florence Mills! Daddy talks about that funeral all the time."

"Really? Anyhow Syl and I had never heard of her."

"Oh yes. They call her 'Blackbird.'"

"We followed her funeral procession up Seventh Avenue to 145th Street. An airplane circled low and released a flock of black birds. They fluttered overhead a few seconds and then flew away."

"Yes, but why did you leave Bermuda to come here?"

"One day I'm going back. One day I'm going back to my country," said Mommi in a voice I never heard before.

"What about your husband, Mr. Feral? How did you meet him?"

"Percy? Him and Syl and I grew up together in Hamilton. He came a courting Syl but I knew he would do for a husband. I wanted someone who would work a steady job. Someone who wouldn't give me any trouble."

"You mean he was courting your sister and you married him. What did she say?"

"Syl? She sewed me the most beautiful wedding dress. She chose the most exquisite lace and the heaviest satin we could afford and encrusted them with tiny seed pearls."

"When did you become a Foster Mother?"

"Why not. I got a green thumb with babies. Babies are no trouble. The dinner was grand, wasn't it?"

"Since the Depression, I guess?"

"Back then, the babies came and went and didn't stay long. The longest any one ever stayed was for three or four months. Times have changed. Nowadays, it's different. There's a new breed of girls coming out of the South. Worthless. The kind of girl who unloads her baby with me, keeps on stepping and never looks back."

23

Daddy eased away from our house noiselessly as an autumn leaf floating to the ground. He attended Sunday dinner promptly at three P.M., sitting in his chair at the head of our table, so it was a while before I realized that his clothes were all gone. Since *that day* we avoided one another. He was an ethereal presence hovering on the edges of my consciousness and now his absence is like a missing painting on the wall that leaves a faint and dusty outline.

One day, at the beginning of my monthly period, I stand, as usual, in Aunt Syl's room waiting for my monthly allotment of sanitary napkins. Daddy doesn't live here any more does he, I blurt out. Without a word, as if I'd never spoken, Aunt Syl disappears into her closet and extricates a record jacket with a man's smiling face on the cover. Underneath his picture written in roses is "John McCormack sings Arias and Art Songs." Aunt Syl stands motionless before the Victrola as his high sweet voice serenades her.

> *Who is Sylvia*
> *What is she*
> *That all our swains command her?*

She studies the picture of the tenor, his glossy black hair, his smiling eyes, and closes her eyes as she bows her head.

Holy fair and wise is she
The heavens with such grace did lend her
That adored she might be
Adored she might be.

"Franz Schubert," she whispers dreamily, "Shooo Burrrr," she says trying to sound German.

Is she kind as she is fair?
For beauty lives with kindness
Then to Sylvia let us sing
She excels each mortal thing
To her garlands let us bring
To her garlands let us bring.

I am no longer in the room as she she studies the picture of the smiling Irish tenor's glossy black hair, smiling eyes, and closes her eyes and bows her head. Her soft, thin, black hair is parted in the center. Around her neck she wears a dainty gold chain. Aunt Syl is a reddish version of Mommi with the same generous lips, ample nose, and bushy eyebrows. But there the similarities end. Aunt Syl has a taste for elegant clothes and literature. She is the owner of the only two books in our small bookcase, *The Little Minister* and *Kingsblood Royal.* And everyone knows that Aunt Syl, after sipping two or three rum and cokes from the red and black striped high-ball glasses, will recite sweetly,

Loveliest of trees, the cherry now
Is hung with bloom along the bough
And stands about the woodland ride
Wearing white for Eastertide.

It was from Aunt Syl that I learned my Bible stories, for she was my Sunday School teacher. On Sunday morning, I sat, a pupil in her Sunday School class, as she instructed me in the Episcopal catechism and prepared me for my Confirmation:

Aunt Syl: What do we learn from the Ten Commandments?
Me: Our duty to God and our neighbors.
Aunt Syl: What are those duties?
Me: To believe, trust, and obey Him.
            To honor and help our parents and family.
            To honor those in authority and to meet their just
            demands.
Aunt Syl: What is the Communion of Saints?
Me: The living and the dead, those whom we love and
            those whom we hurt bound together by sacrament,
            prayer, and praise.

But between the biblical stories and the catechism, much has changed between us. I am twelve now and she is fifty and outside of Sunday School class there are only accusations from her, which I answer with defiant words and angry silences. Without rancor, and with Christian good will, Aunt Syl cautions Mommi about my prominent behind. As I approach puberty, her voice and Mommi's rise in a maniacal duet, and although she mostly follows Mommi's lead, Aunt Syl sometimes takes a solo flight and becomes a virtuoso in her arias of carping criticisms and dire predictions. For her, my ripening body is proof enough of that I am indeed headed for trouble.

One look at my left-handedness, the space between my teeth, which, she says are sure sign of wantonness coupled with my ripening breasts and full, round behind, is sufficient to prompt Aunt Syl to prognosticate that I will indeed follow in May Anna's footsteps. I look at her prim and square figure, her fanaticism about cleanliness, her fear of flesh and sensuality, and understand without being able to articulate it that I am an affront to her because she knows that one day I will open my legs wide, lift them to the stars, and roar in sexual ecstasy.

She is truly perplexed when I am less than grateful for my "lot."

"You should fall down on your knees and be thankful for your lot. A foster child like you should be grateful it was your lot to be taken in by a class of family like ours. "

"Aunt Syl, I need a napkin now," I say urgently, as the blood begins to snake down my legs. Whenever I am in need of a sanitary napkin I have to come to her in her big bare gloomy room where a dark, mammoth four-poster threatens to take over completely.

"'Late again, aren't you?" she asks in an innocent and pleasant voice, as if her question holds no hidden implications. She carefully puts her treasured record down. She is almost innocent and childlike in her questioning. The sanitary box is kept in the rear of the closet behind lots of heavy coats in a plain brown wrapper next to the gallon jugs of Chateau Martin ruby port wine, and as Aunt Syl dives into the deep closet and rummages around, her muffled voice continues in wavy tones.

"When I was your age, my period always arrived on time."

Here we go again, I think.

"Our family owned land back in Bermuda."

"Yes," I mimic silently. *"And you had white folks doing your laundry."*

"And white folks did our laundry. But that was long ago when there were no vehicles or roads in our parish. Our Mother taught my sister and I many things: How to hold our heads up and pass folks by when we know they are talking about us; how to walk on Sundays to the Anglican Church and sit in our rented pews; never to trust a Britisher, the same rule applies to all men; filth, smelliness, and dust is really Lucifer so a woman must watch out, Satan is always trying to settle in her house and on her body; turpentine, onions, vinegar and horehound boiled down close leaves a good syrup for coughs; when doves coo mournfully rain is coming, and a menstruating woman's touch on your plants can kill them dead."

"Whew!" Aunt Syl declares breathless from speech and rummaging around in her cavernous closet and finally emerges clutching a huge, unwieldy box. "I used to have my period once, before my operation. I had it taken out. Doctors agreed that since I wasn't going to use any of those female things it was best to get rid of it before they started to give me trouble. I didn't mind losing them. In fact after what happened—when my mother Winnie was sent away . . ."

"What happened to Mommi? Why was she sent away?"

Aunt Syl continues, "Furthermore, the way women have to bring new life into the world—You know, I had a suitor once. In my time," Aunt Syl muses, "I have been pursued."

Aunt Syl caresses the napkin as if it were exquisite fabric, she examines the cheesecloth, getting lost in its complex threading as if it were intricate lace, she rubs it against her face as if it was the softest velvet.

"We didn't have these back in my day. We had special rags, which we had to wash out in a pail out in the back yard away from everyone's sight."

I stand silently, grimly, as the blood runs down the inside of my leg.

"I know you want me to move away so you can have Winnie all to yourself but I just want you to know, Winnie and I will always be together. I don't even cash my check. She gives me an allowance just like she does Percy. That's the way the three of us made it in New York ever since when we first came. Virginia . . . I . . . am . . . family."

A dam inside breaks. Blood rushes forth and soaks the toilet paper in my panties.

"When Percy came around he was courting me but it didn't really matter because Winnie and I would never break up to go live alone with a man. Especially after what happened to her. Sisters are constant," Aunt Syl continues. "No matter how fat or grey or ill we become, we can count on each other no matter how we look. What human man can offer us that? How could I forget that, especially after what happened to Winnie."

"What happened to her?" I repeat. "What happened to Mommi?

Why was she sent away when she was young? Tell me. I want to know."

"Here's your pad." As I stretch out my hand to take the thick cotton wad our fingers touch. Our eyes meet.

"Where is Daddy?" I ask again.

She looks at me and says, "There's nothing wrong in this house, you hear? Be decent. You see, we are a respectable family. Never any scandal of any kind. No loose women. No jailbirds. No divorce. No bastards. We have to be able to hold up our heads when we walk down the street so nobody can talk bad about us. Remember, the worst thing you can do to Winnie is to publicly disgrace her name, to cause her neighbors to laugh at her when she walks down the street. It would kill her."

24

Octavia. Theodosia. Fredonia. DaVera. Middy. Cherry. Coral. Chloe. Names that seem to urge a tongue to slip into a song. On Sundays and special occasions we wore Gibson Girl blouses with taffeta skirts, red fox nylons, and low thick "Cuban" heels, while on school days, white socks and ox-blood loafers with new pennies, or white buck shoes and pastel-colored imitation leather jackets. When we polished our nails clear pink, we carefully left an unpainted half moon at the cuticles. Our tightly curled poodle cuts and bone-straight pageboys required biweekly touch-ups with the hot irons. Most of our mothers traditionally handed down hope chests they had brought with them to New York, hewn from woods of the Carribean, mahogany, cedar, or the south, Georgia pine, or Virginia oak, that we filled with aprons and pot holders and lace doilies made in Home Economics classes. Our families had not yet escaped to Long Island and we lived between Lenox and Eighth Avenues from 110th to 145th Streets and traveled on the IRT subway downtown to Julia Richmond, Washington Irving, and Textile High or uptown to George Washington: high schools where counselors unfailingly steered each one of us toward General Certificates and Commerical tracks and away from college-oriented Academic Diplomas.

We knew we were not the high yellow girls of the Debutante

Balls and Sororities. Not children of doctors and, in the main, ebony hued, we knew that our assets in the mating market were limited and fleeting: a high school diploma that would assure a prospective husband of our employability, and the purity and youthfulness of the thing between our legs.

Shamelessly, we were marched straight ahead to the day we would cash in our bargaining chips. We had been warned since the onset of puberty that a black girl's path is peppered with land mines and that one wrong move, one misstep, could blow a decent girl to pieces. Our obedient, pious demeanor and brown eyes masked our budding lust, our sanctimonious behaviour under adult gaze belied our lustful daydreams as we sang Anglican hymns in sparkling blue and white choir robes.

We listened to Dr. Jive and Symphony Sid on the south end of our radios and among ourselves would turn any clear space into an instant ballroom and practice our latest dance steps. We sang at Sunday morning Communion services, marched in church processionals and sat in the choir loft in full view of the congregation. We were St. Martin's vestal virgins, a choir of innocence and adolescent beauty, carefully guarded lest some thief gobble up our maidenheads without ritual and ring, ceremony and contract.

Even though we still loved to jump Double Dutch or play dodge ball, we were told we were now too old for such activities. It was almost time for us to catch a subway downtown and look for a job, for soon there would be children to bear and men to keep house for. Underneath our veneer of streetwise sass and urban smarts we were girlish, vulnerable, trusting, and hopeful.

Left to ourselves, we loved to play at being blasphemous and vulgar; we swore a lot.

"Well blow me down and call me shorty and kiss my black ass four times forty, look at who is the fuckin new choir girl," said tall, skinny Octavia on the day of my first choir rehearsal.

"Goddamn . . . girl, listen," continued Octavia, "I had your Aunt for a Sunday school teacher last year and she failed me. Imagine getting a D in Sunday School! How come your mother let you join the Junior Choir? From what I hear she—"

"Shut up Octavia," commanded Theodosia, who was giving out the hymn books. "She can't help it if her mother is kinda strict and crazy."

The old childhood loyalty rose in my throat but instead I heard myself say aloud for the first time, "My mother is dead. Mrs. Feral is my foster mother."

"I don't care who she is, she still crazy. Here is your hymen, oops, I mean hymnal," said Octavia as she handed me a large-cloth covered red book with a gold cross engraved in its center.

"Imagine failing me in Sunday School," Octavia appealed to me again. "What's wrong with your aunt? Is she crazy too? No one fails anybody in Sunday school."

"That's probably because you think that the Holy Trinity was some kind of orgy," answered the girl next to her.

"Oh yeah?" wailed Octavia tossing her hymnal to the concrete floor, wiggling her hips, rolling her eyes to the tin ceilings stamped green squares as she wailed,

> Don't want Jesus in my bed
> Want Mr. Jelly Roll
> To fill my soul instead.
> Want the Holy Ghosts
> With the mostest
> Sanctified and Holy Moly
> Blessed Trinity
> C'mon and do it to me!

When the laughter died down, Theodosia handed me a robe, saying, "You gotta launder this funky thing real good cause all these pious bitches think of while they singing is dick and pussy."

"O Gawd," wailed Octavia, "Forgive me for my holy lust when I'm at the Communion rail on my knees with my mouth wide open waiting for the body of the host and those fine acolytes and young priests are towering over me . . . Talk is cheap. None of you would know what to do if a dick slapped you in the face with an orgasm," said Freddie, a flat-chested girl with close-cropped hair, as she put her arms around me.

"Uh oh, watch out for Freddie," counseled pigeon-breasted Middy, who was reputed to be the only one in the choir who had a good voice. "What goes on under those choir robes is sinful," said Middy.

"Shhh, better not let Mr. Dale Sissy Lips hear you."

"Ole Dale sissy lips jelly lips and tittie tips, wide hips is veddy veddy propah. Some says that he likes the boys, that's why he's the girls' Junior Choirmaster cause the best watch dog over water is oil, " said a fake British accent belonging to pale yellow girl called DaVera.

All this time, coffee-colored Coral, with round, mournful eyes, even when she managed a smile, had been quietly observing the entire ritual, looking on but not laughing or joining in.

She walked over to us, smiling but not friendly. Her immaculate clothes and groomed condition made me aware of my natural state of disarray with braids coming apart, ashy legs, and blouse crawling away from a twisted skirt. She was older than the rest of us and commanded us in a superior voice. "Don't forget to tell her about Clarence."

"OooooOh Clarence," they chorused.

"Don't let him get you in his old blue Mercury," Coral said. I wondered about the needles of tension in her voice. Her rosebud lips were in a perpetual pout. It was difficult to discern whether she was being sullen or sexy. Around her clung an annoying smell of jasmine, sweet, cloying, musky, deep, almost funky.

"He's got a car?" I was incredulous. No one had cars, he must be rich, I thought as I backed away from her scent.

"He thinks the junior choir is his private harem," warned Coral, looking at me closely. "He likes to put each choir girl to the test."

"Not me," I said, the boy space within me anticipating meeting him.

"That's what they all say," Coral murmured as Mr. Dale entered the room.

When choir practice finally began, I sang passionately, loudly, and out of tune, and was immediately relegated to sing second soprano. Still, I loved the music, the navy blue choir robes, with circular starched white collars, the smell of the aged hymnals, the wooden pews, the camaraderie of girls my own age.

—

"I see a new angel has joined the choir. Are you a pure angel or a devil angel?" teased a giant looming above me, leaning on his broom and watching me climb the church stairs for choir practice one day.

"I hear you are a virgin. Are you?"

"Ask your momma," I retorted weakly, flooded by awkwardness, shyness, anger, and shame. I wasn't used to banter with boys. All I could see was a brown bulk gawking at me as I continued up the church stairs.

"Yeah, you one," he concluded, turning his back on me as he resumed sweeping the church steps. "I can tell."

Nearing the top step I could see that he wasn't really a brown giant but almost. I liked his bulkiness.

"Who are you?" I asked, pulling my hand from his. There was a golden nimbus around his large head from the light on the church door.

"You must be the new girl. Don't worry. All the girls in the junior choir are virgins . . . when they first join." He bent down to sweep the dust into a dustpan and his thighs made me think of tree trunks.

"Who the hell are you?"

"I'm Clarence, the church sweeper, the keys-keeper, the chief acolyte and mainly here to keep you fine choir angels satisfied and pure. That's who I am."

"You are a fool, fool," I laughed, looking past his glasses into his nearsighted eyes that gave him a penetrating stare, appreciating his thick slab of moist brown lips, his slew feet, the way his big frame filled the air with his massiveness, and his comic-book goofiness. A brown comic book Archie, I smiled to myself.

"Bet you can't even take company," Clarence challenged.

"O yes I can," I lied.

"Everybody knows you can't. Everybody knows you're Mrs. Feral's foster girl and she won't let you out. But don't worry, I'll get you out of the house," he promised.

"Oh yeah," I laughed angrily. "How you gonna do that?"

"I'm The Mothers' Friend. I know how to make mothers trust me. I will call on Mrs. Feral and ask her for permission to take you out on your first official date."

"It's a waste of time. No."

"Don't worry, I'll get you out of the house," he promised again.

He stared at me for a long time. "You have nice eyes."

I marveled at his admiration. No boy had ever talked to me before. At least not like this.

"And that tain't all," he continued, sweeping his eyes slowly over my body.

My voice sounded full and throbbing in my own ears as I murmured, "You are very fresh."

"Rather be fresh than stale."

Standing on the church steps with the afternoon dimming fast around us, I was sixteen years old and aware of nothing in the world except the boy in front of me with heavy-lidded eyes that looked as if they were half-closed in prayer, whose large feet looked rooted, steady, and permanent, and whose big hands and large square body looked to me a strong and safe buttress.

"Virginia-The-Virgin," he chanted, "is-early-the choir-room-is-locked-I-have-the-keys. Come-with-me." His lips were full and large as if he knew the immense power of the spoken word.

I follow him through the church entrance, down the stairs to the dark choir room, our footsteps hollow sounds against the gray concrete floors. His keys clang noisily in the silence. The door finally opens. The grand piano is a lurking behemoth in the dark. We need no words. We are on primal ground and know what to expect from each other as we step into the dance gracefully, naturally. His laughing eyes are playful and determined; mine are joyful, willing but hesitant. He touches my cheek, I rest my hand on his shoulder. He touches my right breast and I let his hand rest there a moment before I lift it and hold it in mine; he lifts my dress; I rub my nose against the grains of hair on his chin. His fingers, one at a time, crawl lazily up my thighs. I stream, my insides liquid, before I push his hand away. He chases me and we play tag among the choir benches, his scent mingles with the mustiness of aged wood and yellowing hymn books, his scent rises like the heat and smoke of church candles and I stumble, let him catch and touch me again and again while I smile and pull toward him, then back away from him, all the time sighing and breathing, "No."

Bright lights flood the room as loud footsteps clatter down the stairs and it was time to begin choir practice. I know that whatever other coupling, whatever other act of love I may experience in the years ahead, these moments would always be my first time.

⌐

Every Saturday afternoon from two P.M to seven P.M. teenagers could dance at the Savoy Ballroom, but headliners like Cootie Williams and Art Tatum were saved for the adult evening crowd. Two marble staircases curled up to the second level and led to the dance floor. On a wall mural, hovering like guardian angels, were two smiling women, a mulatto wearing a blue dress, and an ebony one in flaming red. In between them a blue-black sheik smiled down upon the teenage dancers, who were elegantly patting, jumping, kicking, driving, dragging, shuffling, stomping, snapping, and singing to the jazz rhythms of a swinging but unknown band. Diamond flecks of light spilled from a large cut-glass chandelier and spotted our bodies and faces. Reverently, we entered the sacred space of the dance floor, endless miles of maple wood with a glass sheen.

Clarence rhythmically two-steps towards me and lifts me over his head. Suspended in midair, the blast of the saxophone merges with the thud of Mrs. Feral's backhand slap; the piano notes slither into my giggles born of purple bruises and blood-clotted fingernails; the plaintive trumpets spiral into the incandescent glow of Teddie's eyes and the gold fingernails of an old man on top of a white horse, and sink into low moans in an empty church as fast, thick drumbeats become a percussive blanket that shields a naked foster father stretched at the bottom of an electric cross, until finally, the walking bass congeals it all into a longing for a lost mother for whom there is no image, touch, or smell.

When Clarence swung me to the floor, I slid between his legs, and our quivering bodies pulsated in time with the shivering, syncopated tones exulting in the air. We were filled with the regenerative force of music; each note was a new cell in our bodies, and I knew that our movements were not about exhibitionism or expertness but simply a belief in dancing as a force of life.

In the center of the dance floor, in the eye of an ecstatic yell as bodies twirled and leapt and spun, I suddenly found myself looking into the baleful eyes, pouty mouth, and somber face of Coral, staring at us as she danced in an amorphous circle of boys and girls without any specific partner.

"Isn't the band cooking?" she said, looking past me at Clarence. My nostrils quivered at her thick jasmine scent. As soon as Clarence spied her he missed a step, became clumsy, awkward, then quickly regained his rhythm all in a few beats.

"Remember what I told you," she managed to hiss in my ear before a surge of music and writhing bodies swallowed her up and pushed her forward like flotsam in a tidal wave.

"What did Coral say to you?" Clarence asked while we were dancing the slow drag to *Mood Indigo.*

"Is she your girlfriend?" I whispered.

His back stiffened. "Our families are friends."

"Do you, like her, I mean."

"I talk to her. I talk to a lot of girls. I'm talking to you now."

Reassured, I turned toward the music. I couldn't believe I was dancing at the Savoy Ballroom. There was only Clarence and me and the music.

My joy made walking from 140th Street and Lenox Avenue to 120th Street a stroll through paradise. In an arc of water gushing from an open fire hydrant there were glistening rainbows. Our laughter made the sidewalks fields of new mown grass under our feet. We were rose-colored in the hues of a salmon sunset. Human voices and traffic sounds melted into a continuation of the jazz still inside of us. "You're a good dancer," Clarence smiled down at me through his thick glasses. "So are you," I murmured softly. "So are you."

⟋

BAM! A metal buckle cracks against my cheekbone as soon as he is halfway down the stairs.

"You bastard!" she screams, "let me see your panties!" WHAP! "What are those white stains on them? Why do you smell that way? Why are your clothes all wrinkled? Stop stinking up my house with your mother's whorish ways!"

Much later in my room I hear them discussing the shocking headlines. Daddy, Aunt Syl, Rose, and Teddie, and Mommi's voices skim over the surface of my loud sobs.

"Drowned him."

"Cut his head off like he was a chicken."

"Found him in the bottom of the Mississippi River."

"Boy? Teenager?"

"Shot him too."

"Lord today. White folks."

"Who is that young fool anyhow?"

"Some boy Emmett Till. Said he was looking at a white woman."

"He should know better."

"Acorn acting like a big oak in the wrong forest."

"Body in the bottom of the Mississippi."

"His own mother didn't recognize him."

"Hmmmm. Mmmmm. White folks, something else, ain't they?"

"Cut off his head, shot and drowned him."

"Beat him and tore off his head. Hmmmmmm."

"White folks cruel ain't they?"

"Cowards too. Boy not yet a man. A child."

"A child Lord Jesus. Just a child."

"The Book say Suffer little children to come unto me."

"I don't understand how anyone could do such a thing . . . and to a child."

―

I invent a running set of lies. How could I tell her that after Sunday School in his 1950 blue Mercury, fragrant with the aroma of his sex and his Pall Malls, in any tree-shaded quiet area I let his fingers gingerly test my fresh bruises for infected blood as his tongue licked my scarred and scabby back and he plied me with his fingers?

Come Sundays, my pleasure with him began at eight A.M. Communion Service when he led the processional, lumbering between the aisles, filling the church with white puffs of incense from his swinging censer. I followed him in sparkling choir robes, chanting and singing, marching onto the inlaid marble floor of the Sanctuary, to the twenty-three-foot High Altar ornamented by beautiful mosaic. Forty-five boring minutes later I trailed behind Clarence again as he now leads the recessional, retracing our steps along the same route. I am restless through the Sunday School hours, the wooden recitation of catechisms and psalms and Bible stories, thinking only of the back seat of his car in some Harlem lover's lane.

We meet secretly every Sunday down through the church calendar.

On Advent Sunday, from the floor of his car, Mount Morris's black rocks loom like volcanic mountains. On Ephiphany Sunday, from a secluded underpass on Riverside Drive, New Jersey weaves in and out of the fog like a mirage as we watch the George Washington Bridge vanish into the January mist. On Harlem Heights, on the first Sunday in Lent, breath-fogged car windows reveal bony trees thrusting fingers of skeletal branches into a bleak winter sky. The scented lilies of Whitsunday are seen everywhere in Central Park North from our secret car parked between the trees on 110th Street and 7th Avenue. On Trinity Sunday, in Morningside Park, his fingers make me tremble and I tip over into a stream of ecstasy.

Whenever Clarence touches me, I am free of Mommi. He is a weapon and a shield. I place my hands on his penis. His semen leaks and pools in my palm. "You know I'm on my way to Korea," Clarence pleads. "Just the tip. I promise I won't push it in all the way." I almost fall over the edge as he parts my thighs but I always find the strength to snap my legs shut. Aching and groaning with lust, I always find the strength to quickly push Clarence away. Aching and groaning with lust I always moan, No, No, No, because Mommi's voice is stronger than even my adolescent lust and Clarence's blue Mercury is only a crucible where I will hang on to my hymen in order to redeem May Anna's blood and prove I am not the slut my foster mother says is in my blood; I am not the harlot of her prophecies.

25

Sundays were full of unfulfilled lust, guilt, and church music. Always, in the tintinnabulation of bells as they swell in the air, I hear our choirmaster Mr. Dale's commanding mantra, "Let it flow let it flow let it flooooow." His face takes shape in the unfurling notes, his liquid mouth in a perfect circle, his eyes fixed on the ceiling as his hand move through the air like undulating waves as he liltingly instructs "Lllleeet it floooooW!"

His moon face is luminous before me, radiant and wet with tears in a moment when he is "with music."

Many legends swirled about him. He had perfect pitch. He was his own tuning fork and tuned our choir piano every single day using his own inner scale. He was a person of clefs and measures, sharps and flats, and was no longer human whenever he was playing at the piano or singing at one of his frequent concerts. Gravity no longer imprisoned him, he became one with the music that poured from him, flooded the room, floated through the walls and windows, and rolled through the church. When he finished he would look all around the room in a distracted manner, surprised to find himself and others in it.

He could see the color of a musical note.

"Orange, girls, orange! How many times must I tell you C

sharp is orange with shimmering lights shining through. Can't you see it?" he would yell at us when we sang a wrong note.

He was called a sissy. "When you gonna find yourself a girl?" was a teasing question he was frequently asked. "I'm looking for one whose pitch is as perfect as mine," he would laugh, and throw his head back as if he had just told an enormous joke.

Church lore said he had gone to England to study liturgical music. Others said that at one time he had been an opera singer of some renown. He had even, some said, once won a scholarship to a famous European conservatory but returned prematurely to America because he had been disappointed. It was never explained by who or what but only that the disappointment was strong enough to cause him to retreat to St. Martin's and devote his solitary life to music. Yes, he's an eccentric, church members whispered, but you have to understand. The poor man was disappointed.

It was rumored that he was a distant relative of Roland Hayes or Marion Anderson. No one ever knew where he lived. We thought maybe in the choir room in the basement or the choir loft in the chapel since he was always there, playing the piano or the organ, his portly figure dressed in his black practice choir robe and his face rigid with music and luminous from the sweat of inspiration.

Choirmaster, organist and soloist, respected, deferred to, talked about in low whispers and snickers, Mr. Dale always remained above any tempest he caused, and at St. Martin's, music was his fiefdom and he was an imperious ruler.

"We need a bell," he announced at a parish meeting one evening.

"Our church has a great iron cross on a church tower 90 feet above the ground with a magnificent spire. But what is a church tower without a bell?" Mr. Dale continued, his sonorous voice riding smoothly over the covert ridicule.

Pandemonium broke loose in the sacristy. The cane-back chairs were pushed and scraped noisily on the pine floors as one after the other the parishoners leapt out of their seats to speak.

"Are you crazy? A church bell in Harlem? "

"Well, why not? In my island I'customed to be called to worship by a bell."

"Yeah, well this ain't your island."

"But it's my home. I a citizen now."

"Look, Small Island, we in Manhattan now. When you gonna get it though your coconut brain that Manhattan Island ain't in the Carribean?"

"At the same time you people learn some culture, class, and refinement!"

"We gonna get all that from a bell?"

"We got fire engines yelling and police sirens screaming, ambulances wailing, screeching, and yelling. Who's gonna hear some damn church bells ringing here in Harlem?"

"A church bell costs money!"

"I never let a dollar stand between me and what I want to do. This is for your bell," said Mr. Richman, Clarence's father, who looked around to make sure he had everyone's attention.

Trying not to be impressed, more people streamed toward the choirmaster offering their donations until one of the older boys who was home from a black college in North Carolina protested.

"Why are you all so backward? The whole country is talking about integration and all you can think about is a church bell. We should be boycotting and demonstrating with the rest—"

"Integration?" interrupted Father Broyard, the soft-spoken rector. He discouraged all conversations about race and there was a rumor that his new Jamaican wife with his exact same very light complexion was aghast when a parishioner referred to her and Father Broyard as black.

"My church is an excellent model of integration despite its unfortunate geographic location. Just look at our ecclesiastical architecture and our liturgical art. The rounded arches of our church are based on the tradition of Byzantium, once the center of the civilized world. It is also in the tradition of the Romans, as well as the Saxons who followed them. We have a cross patterned after the Greek Christians, and our beautiful stained glass is from Italy and France where glassblowing is a live tradition. And we have great ties and interest in the traditions of England, the Home of our Church of the Anglican Communion."

"What does that have to do with blackness?" asked the college student.

"This is not a church of social action. We come here only to worship God and obey the laws of our country. 'Render unto Caesar, that which is Caesar's, and unto God, that which is his.'"

"What a pity, to spend such a large sum of money for bells with so many poor people nearby," continued the college student.

"A fat man will shrivel up and die if he has no spiritual food."

"I vote a resounding No. As far as I can see this bell is just some more of Dale's foolish folly."

"And I vote Yes, Yes, Yes," sang out Coral's mother. "What a lovely idea. You can ring them when my daughter Coral gets married."

"I second that," said Clarence's mother as she touched Coral's hand. "When my son takes his bride I want the bells of St. Martin's to ring in blessing of their union." Coral turned around to smile at me as Clarence, seated beside her, looked straight ahead.

The controversy was causing a civil war within our church. In protest against Mr. Dale's "craziness," staunch members left and joined St. Phillip's Church on Sugar Hill, a church reputed to maintain strict color categories where according to Harlem legend the favorite hymn was "None but the Yellow Shall See Gawd."

"The crooks have tried to cheat us and palm off on us ship bells, train bells, even farm bells," wailed determined Mr. Dale during his report at the next parish meeting. "Now I understand first hand, the atmosphere in which Garvey got bamboozled and his Black Star Line white ship captain absconded with the funds. That same kind of atmosphere exists today when black folks try to do something independently."

"You gonna put only one bell in that great big ole tower?" said

someone sarcastically. "For such a big tower we need a slew of bells, ding dong!"

"You're right, we need a carillon," retorted the choirmaster.

"Yeah, just like the one over at Riverside church?" asked the same sarcastic voice.

"They have 78 bells and we don't need that many."

"But that's the Rockefeller church. It's all right to dream high but this is ridiculous. There's not single wealthy person in this church. How can you even . . ."

"I have looked into some second-hand bells."

"You can't make do with something like this. Here's one hundred dollars, Dale, ole man. Nothing's too good for my church," said Clarence's father grandly.

"We could get thirteen bells to ring as a simple chime," offered Mr. Dale humbly.

"Don't get thirteen bells. It's an unlucky number and you will be ringing in your own death knell."

"What about electric chimes, amplified by loudspeakers in the tower? It would be a good imitation."

"Shucks man, we want the real thing if we gonna do it at all. I told you I never let a dollar stand between me and what I want to do. Here's two hundred more dollars—"

"We need bells that are cast accurately enough to play a melody and sound in harmony. There's no foundry in America that does that."

"What about other foundries? Outside America?"

"What about the anti-noise injunction in New York? You know what happens everytime we try to do something?"

"Let 'em try. Just let them try to stop us."

St. Martin's Church Bells became a cause célèbre. The surrounding churches as well as the nearby synagogue got involved. Proprietors from the number holes and corner saloons thought it good politics to contribute. All cooperated and reached out to add something joyful and creative to our neighborhood.

Social life revolved around the Bell Fund. Raffles were sold and bell auctions held. Each person who contributed to the bells would have their names inscribed on them, so family and friends banded together "to get a bell before all the best notes are taken, "as my foster mother declared as she made her payment on a G bell weighing 275 pounds.

Our choirmaster sent an order to a foundry in Holland for a carillon of forty-two bells with the largest one weighing 3200 pounds and the smallest one twenty pounds, and weddings were delayed along with attempts to stave off death until "Mr. Dale's craziness" was installed in the tower.

"Perfectly cast, pure in tone, sonorous in volume," declared the choirmaster when the forty-two bells arrived from Holland, and then he dropped the bombshell. "We are going to have royalty at our little church in Harlem. Queen Juliana of Holland is currently touring the city and has accepted my invitation to be at the carillon installation service!"

The following Sunday, although seven thousand jubilant people are lined in the streets in front of our church, there is a softness in the voices, a mellow feeling the air, an absence of the usual city shrillness.

A barefoot toddler rips off his diaper, breaks away from the hand that holds him, waddles under the wooden barriers and scampers like a chicken into the middle of the street. He stands stock still and holds out his arms to the laughing crowd. A smiling policeman gently leads the naked boy back to his mother. As the hour nears, a blanket of hushed anticipation covers the crowd and the familiar noise of barking dogs, crying babies, cursing men, breaking glass, thumping jukeboxes, clattering truckwheels on asphalt and relentless car horns is muted by our joyous anticipation.

Then the thundering roll of motorcyles crescendoes down Lenox Avenue.

One hundred policeman with the city's orange, blue, and white flags flying from the mastheads of their machines lead a procession of cars and stop in front of St. Martin's. A tiny woman slowly curls out from the cocoon of a long black limousine. Her blue linen suit is wrinkled in the seat of her skirt; she sweats from the July sun; her wispy blonde hair is limp in the July heat. Her round white straw hat is crooked, making her look tipsy as she stretches to her full height. She graciously accepts the flowers presented to her by our Ladies Guild and then unexpectedly bends down to caress the small children nearest to her and whispers something in their ears to make them giggle. Then she looks up straight into the crowd and smiles. She makes eye contact with several adults and says in a clear strong voice, "Thank you for inviting me." Hats lift with a deafening roar of welcome. Then a silence so sudden, so deep I can hear my own heartbeat.

"Look," says someone pointing up to the bell tower.

The choirmaster is a tiny dot floating above us. His voice, amplified through a megaphone, floats down to us.

"Bells petition God to hear our prayers. Bells form a bridge of sound between the spiritual world and this earthly one. From this day on," he declares, "St. Martin's carillon bells are the Privileged Instrument of not only this church but all of Harlem. From this day on it shall establish the pitch standard of all music, religious or secular, played in the village of Harlem!"

"Dig that, now it's official. I always knew God played jazz, and sang the blues," laughs the college student.

A din of incredulity, laughter, amusement, and wonder ripples through the crowd as Mr. Dale sweeps into the tower to play the bell clavier.

And then the ecstatic peal of the bells. Each note the sound of sparkling, clear water. *Swing Low, Sweet Chariot, America the Beautiful, Abide with Me,* spirituals, patriotic songs and hymns, pour down, majestic intimate sounds full of light, rippling gently through the air, falling like silver leaves.

26

Slow as time, weightless white flakes drifted past courtroom windows. Inside, I endured the recesses, intervals, and endless waiting, while outside, white mist dispersed the frail March sunshine. Kelvin lay placid in my arms as if he were hanging on to every word I mumured. Suddenly one by one, sounds, noises that signaled the beginning of something about to happen, a warning rustling that was a signal to me I had little time left to imprint our history upon Kelvin's skin and pour my words through his pores before he was gone, relinquished forever. I held my son high in my arms, his ears to my mouth, and I whispered.

Child, it was not all bad. I was lucky enough to spend my childhood in Harlem during the 1940s and early fifties. The air of my childhood was filled with struggle and music, politics and art. Muses walked in Harlem in the guise of ordinary mortals. Paul Robeson and Ben Davis were regular speakers at my elementary school until the teachers who invited them were dismissed by the Board of Education as "Reds."

However, although everyone else was jitterbugging to Johnny Hodge's 45 r.p.m. "Squaty Root," pledging their love to Johnny Ace, mamboing and cha-cha-ing down at the Palladium on Wednesday evenings, there was nothing worth doing that I could get away with until Norman Lewis, the great Abstract Expressionist painter, walked through our door and brought with him the art and politics going on in Harlem in the early fifties.

27

The outline of tenements cut zigzag patterns in a dim sky. The rain spread a gray, steel-blue-tinged veil on the day I went to the Harlem atelier to summon Norman. Through a rainy haze, a fuzzy afternoon emerged. Starting from 120th Street I walked through a skein of inhabited silence as muted voices and muffled traffic noises and the A flat minor timbre of leaking drainpipes splashed against a background din of falling rain.

At the southeast corner of 125th Street I made an unauthorized stop at the Liggett's Drugstore soda fountain. The hiss of the seltzer machine punctuated the laughing conversation between those seated and the line of customers waiting their turn to sit on the gleaming brass stools.

"What I want with a woman who was a girl when I was a boy?" wheezed an old man as a young waitress handed him a chocolate malted.

"My ole lady is 65 and so am I. That's 130 years in the bed. What I'm gonna do with that?" he asked the waitress who smiled at him with unseeing eyes.

"Hey pops, I'm gonna start drawing the Social Security by the time you finish," said a man behind him as he shifted impatiently from one foot to another.

"Better not take too long with your malted cause the Security won't cover the cost," advised a woman next to me wearing a rain-slicked bright red fur coat.

"Don't study him, baby," grinned the old man showing his toothless gums. "But dahling, you don't have to wait. You can come sit on ole gramp's lap."

Behind the soda fountain were miles of wooden bins of beauty supplies, ladies' underwear, hardware, sewing notions, and greeting cards. Pushed against the wall were refrigerators and radios and bicycles. The prescription counter consisted of aspirins, cigarettes, and candy bars. No one had ever seen a pharmacist.

I abandoned the idea of an ice cream soda and continued uptown. I was excited about seeing this mysterious man I had heard so much about but rarely seen. His father, Wilfred, was my godfather. Having a godfather made me feel legitimate and blood-linked, and in Uncle Wilfred I saw not only my genesis but the beginning of us all. After all, he had been an adult when Mommi and Aunt Syl and Daddy were still children in that mythical land of Bermuda. He had been a groom for their father's horses, according to Aunt Syl. The whites of Uncle Wilfred's eyes were red as if the residue of his silent passions settled there. His chiseled jawbone and livid blue-black flesh transformed his rock-hewn face into an impenetrable ancient mask.

Wilfred Lewis was a silent, bitter man. He had a harsh playfulness about him, but ancient quarrels and years of seething silences pervaded his family life. Godfather had not spoken to his wife for twenty years, although they still lived in the same two-bedroom apartment on 145th Street where they had raised three sons, Sol, Norman, and Johnny. After some long-ago quarrel Uncle Wilfred became Mommi's boarder and ate his meals at our house every night before he returned to his silent apartment. No longer young, he was still a longshoreman on the Brooklyn docks; his stone-carved flesh began to slacken, his step faltered, a cough wracked his body.

Through the years he only mentioned Norman's name with dry

anger in his voice and a curl of scorn on his thick, dark, dry lips, snarling that Norman hung out with "those damn Communists." I couldn't wait to meet him.

At 306 West 141st Street I stood before a large storefront with "Harlem Art School" painted in gold. I noisily opened the door and stepped into a completely quiet room of thirty artists. Thick maroon corduroy draped the large street-level windows, casting a silence and adding to the atmosphere of hushed creative concentration. The men and women sketched quickly, some standing at easels, others sitting with boards in front of them, scrubbing away on their drawing paper, erasing or adding, leaving trails of charcoal smudges on their face and clothes.

Before them, under a bright light, reclined a monumental, fleshy, naked woman looking out into space with a serene unfocused stare like a large, indifferent white cat. The black couch on which the creature stretched voluptuously made her pale skin luminous; her massive arms were stretched behind, cradling her head. This reclining stretching angle accented her globular breasts and mountainous thighs. There was a patch of black curly pubic hair, which her raised left leg and shapely right hand with its tapered fingers failed to conceal. At first sight, my reaction was immediate and primal.

My feet took two steps toward her, in an involuntary effort to draw closer to inhale the musk I imagined she exuded, before I stopped them, and without any warning from deep within something thrilled and burst and liquified. Then, as if by some secret signal, the magnificent creature rose up on her haunches, slipped into a robe, and exited.

I could not restrain myself from looking at their easels, to see how they captured the form and overflowing sensuality of the fertility goddess I had just seen. My eyes flew from easel to easel, but instead of any attempt to duplicate the swollen breasts and sloping buttocks and partially concealed vulva that had moved me to orgasm, there were only lines, and loops and shadow and light.

The artists, one by one, stopped working, rose out of their seats, and began to follow a short, wide-hipped, dark woman with slanted eyes and high cheekbones.

She moved from easel to easel, a trail of students behind her. Stopping in front of an easel spackled with lozenges and triangles of charcoal erupting in thick swatches of squares and rectangles, she commented to the artist standing next to it, "Human mass translated into geometric flights of motion and light, intersecting to make and form."

Turning her head around to the easel that had swirls and swoops of color crescending across its canvas, she smiled and said, "Yes, you got it, that's it, space, light, and movement."

She moved from easel to easel, complimenting, analyzing.

"Never forget that form, color, structure are conten——"

She stopped excitedly, spying an easel with charcoal loops and swirls.

"Over here, see, this is what I mean. I think of Lewis as a musician-painter, for he starts in softly on the blank page, improvising and when he sees a suitable motif, like this eye over here for instance. He refracts it a thousand times, giving it various shapes, swinging his brush with with confidence, playing it up for what it's worth and then, satisfied he has gone the whole way with it permits it, to fade softly out."

Standing by the easel, as if guarding it, was a man I immediately recognized: Godfather Wilfred as a young man. A chocolate man of medium height, Lewis's eyes were huge, round, bottomless, luminous orbs of light so bright you were relieved when he blinked. He listened to to his mentor unblinkingly without comment.

"But, are you saying simple solids are no longer relevant?" asked a goateed man with a beret.

"Solids and spaces are of equal importance. Forces of action and reaction. Expansion and contraction where all is risk. That's the key word, 'risk.'"

Finally, during a break I went over to him and gave him Mommi's note. He read it and then looked at me, his thick moustache quivering with emotion.

"You're one of Mrs. Feral's foster girls."

He was gentle, dignified. There was a slight tremor in his voice escaping from what appeared to be an otherwise calm countenance. His eyes were slightly moist and he looked directly into mine as if we were well acquainted and said, "Come over here where we can talk."

As I followed him to a corner in the quiet room he asked, "How old are you now? "

"Almost fourteen."

"I haven't seen my dad in eight of those fourteen years."

"Why?" I already knew the answer.

"He thinks I'm a bum."

"He's ill now."

"I'm still a bum."

"Are you gonna come to the house?"

"Tell me, what do you do?"

What did I do? Want kind of question was that? Nobody had ever asked me that. I go to school. I come home. I try to stay out of Mommi's way.

"I read," I replied.

"What?"

"Dostoevsky, Dickens, O'Henry's Short Story, D. H. Lawrence, Bernard Shaw, John Steinbeck, Langston Hughes, Arna Bontemps, Grimm's Fairy Tales, Molière and Racine," stretching the truth a little because I had not gotten to them yet but intended to.

"One day soon you must tell me what you think about them," Lewis said in a voice that made me vow to hurry up and read them before he asked me about them again.

"Know anything about art?"

"A little," I continued to lie. "Michelangelo, Mona Lisa. Rembrandt, Van Gogh."

"Good, have you ever heard of Motley, Bannister, Hale Wood-ruff, Aaron Douglas, and Elisabeth Catlett and Prophet?"

"No."

"These are celebrated Negro painters, in Europe."

"Oh."

"Did you ever try painting?"

"Not since I was little."

"Try it. Just smear some color on a surface. Color is a religious experience."

I had never heard anyone talk like that and certainly not to me. I loved color also. But his unblinking limpid eyes made me nervous as he looked at me for what seemed an eternity.

"Does my father want to see me? Did he say so? Did he send you?"

"Mommi sent me. Are you coming? What shall I say?"

Norman was so busy staring at my hands he couldn't answer. Too late, I tried to hide the swollen knuckles, the blood-tattooed fingernails of the third and fourth fingers of my left hand.

He grabbed my left hand and turned it over, examining each mashed and blood-clotted fingernail.

"I see you are left-handed," he said, letting my hand drop quickly.

"Sometimes. When I'm not thinking," I answered as the class started filing back to their easels.

"I'll come," he said, walking toward his easel. He stopped and stood still, looking me as if he wanted to study me from a distance.

"I'll come," he repeated, as he started to walk away again and then tossed over his shoulder the words, "three o'clock on Sunday."

―

On Sunday, Norman Lewis stood in our doorway and introduced the magnificent nude I had seen in his art class, "This is Stella." I had been right. She had a fragrance of natural sensuality. Everything about her was soft, including her flowing clothes in muted mauves, blues, and greens, colorful and flowing. Her imposing presence energized and illuminated Norman. When Stella shook my hand, she smiled, looked into my eyes, and purred throatily, "Glad to meet you. Norman's been talking about you every day since you came to the class." I fell in love.

When Norman Lewis came to dinner he was already a renowned painter in both uptown and downtown galleries, with many solo exhibitions that were reviewed in major art magazines, and had recently been included in a show of abstract painters in America at the Museum of Modern Art.

However, that Sunday on 120th Street, he was merely an errant son presenting an obligatory guest offering when he presented Mommi with a small painting that he had framed. On a background awash with a fading sunset melting into murky moonlight, drawn in ink, were myriads of tiny, triangular people, in crowds, in small groups, and alone, people advancing in the same direction, swarming like insects to some point beyond the perimeters of the canvas.

"Flight," he had written over his signature N.L.

For years, when someone peering closely at the ~~painting~~, trying to find something familiar, asked, "But ~~what's~~ it supposed to be?" Mommi would chuckle. Eventually, she did come to understand his importance in the art world enough to stop saying "Norman's mess" out loud.

Conversation swirled around the long mahogany dining table as the turkey, bursting with stuffing from the open cave between its drumsticks, was brought in on a silver platter.

"A rally at Carnegie Hall for the Rosenbergs," said Norman. "Wouldn't you like to attend?" Of course I would, but what was the use? I knew I wouldn't be allowed.

"They'll be lots of young people there from high schools all over New York," added Stella, looking directly at Mrs. Feral.

"Lots of young Communists," growled Norman's father.

"Yes," said Stella, "and also Socialists and Democrats and Catholics and Jews. We don't discriminate. Anybody can join our

Committee to Free Ethel Rosenberg." Ethel Rosenberg's plain face and woeful expression on the front pages flashed before me as the conversation flowed and ebbed.

"The husband and wife atom bomb spies?"

"The electric chair just 'cause she's a Jew."

"The electric chair. Her and her husband."

"Her two little boys.

"Just because she's a Jew."

I thought about Ethel Rosenberg's quill hat and gray box over-coat with black velvet collar similar to Mommi's and Aunt Syl's, as under Daddy's gleaming carving knife slices of meat fell like cards.

"Who gets the pope's nose this time?" Daddy asked, looking at me. Wanting to appear mature I said, "Let Teddie have it."

"Out of one war, into another. This time it's Korea."

"Damn Truman."

"Ever notice how its always brown or yellow or red . . . never white."

"Nazis were white."

"Rally. Paul Robeson, Ossie Davis, Ruby Dee. Town Hall."

"Damn Communists."

"No thank you. I'm a vegetarian," said Stella when Mommi passed her the platter of steaming meat.

"You are? I'm a Scorpio," I piped up, taking advantage of Norman's presence to dare join in the adult conversation.

"That means that she doesn't eat any meat," explained Norman. "Neither do I."

"Oh." It was the first time I had heard of such a thing.

"Strayed a long way from your roots," grumbled Godfather Wilfred, looking at his son.

"I didn't know, Stella. I can fix you something else," said Mommi, alarmed.

"O Winnie just pass the damn turkey!" Godfather Wilfred growled.

"Don't go to any bother. I 'll just have some of your delicious collards," reassured Stella.

"Has it got ham hocks in it?" asked Norman.

"Yes," Mommi wailed as she rushed into the kitchen.

"This Korean mess is good for the economy."

"No white meat, no white gravy, no white bread, no vanilla ice cream. No white food." Godfather Wilfred spoke to no one in particular as he meticulously chose all dark meat, pushing the white slices to the side,

"I know what you mean, Mr. Lewis," said Stella, her blue eyes bristling. "I'm not a white bread person either." And then slowly taking Lewis's dark hand into her white one she continued, "I've always liked my toast well done. Dark, almost burnt."

Godfather went into a prolonged fit of coughing.

In the kitchen, her culinary reputation at stake, Mommi rushed around preparing something for her vegetarian guests, while at the table Godfather was still choking on Stella's retort and Daddy vigorously pounded his back as he sputtered and coughed.

"Here, drink this," said Norman, handing his father a glass of water and trying not to laugh. Then he turned to Rose and asked her, "Do you still play the piano?"

"Sometimes. Not like I used to. I'm taking a business course."

"What about your music?"

"Soon as I learn the dictaphone machine and pass my steno course I'm taking the civil service exam."

"So young and so hopelessly middle class."

"Somebody has to have a job. Your brother Solomon is a detective now," said Godfather, fully recovered.

Aunt Syl proudly passed around her famous biscuits.

"Good. If I know Sol he's getting plenty of graft money. At least you got one successful son," said Norman, taking a biscuit from his plate.

"You haven't answered. Would you like to come to the rally?" asked Stella. "Lots of young people your age work with us."

I hung my head and kept silent.

"Communists," repeated Godfather disgustedly.

"Pops. Think about the Scottsboro Boys or the Trenton Six. That's what this is. Only difference is they're Jews."

"Where are the Communists every time the Black Nationalists try to integrate 125th Street?"

"Black Nationalists? You mean your cronies on the corner standing on the soapbox still fighting the Italian-Ethiopian War?"

"Black and white unity, Mr. Lewis. That's all we're interested in," added Stella.

"In my book that means business as usual. White over black."

"In our book it is one world."

"Why that world got to be white? Why can't it be its original black color?"

"What's wrong with brown?"

"Brown is neither fish nor fowl."

"First true thing you said all night. We are talking about human beings."

"So am I. Just look at nature. You see a brass monkey trying to be a swan? You Communists use the black man. No one is for the black man but the black man!"

Mommi rushed in with a folded golden omelet and placed it before Stella and Norman.

"Eggs for dinner?" I thought. "Yuck."

Suddenly a hush as Mommi bowed her head. "Norman, grace the table, if you please."

"Who should I thank?" inquired Norman.

"The Man upstairs, of course," said Mommi.

"How about thanking the Man of the House?"

"Norman, don't start in with your foolish Communist talk."

"ThanktheLordforthisfoodthatweareaboutoreceive Amen. Let's eat!" said Mommi, hoping to avoid a religious discussion.

"Good," said Norman. "Now instead of thanking some ghost up in the sky, I would now like for all of us to bow our heads and thank your husband for going out to Jersey every morning and enduring told and untold indignities to put food on this table."

Instead of bowing his head, Norman lifted a glass of wine in the air and chanted:

> Why praise a spook high in the sky
> You'll only see him when you die
> Before you sits a flesh and blood man
> Whom we should thank whenever we can
> Though quiet in his appointed seat
> It is he who brings forth the meat.
> So Glory and Hallejuah
> Monsieur Feral, All praises are due ya!

Daddy humbly bowed his head, visibly moved. An appreciative giggle escaped my lips, but Mommi shot me a thunderbolt that glued my lips.

"And," Norman continued, "I would like to thank Aunt Winnie and Aunt Syl because

> Mealtime is a Sacrament
> Food carefully cooked
> And beautifully presented is an Art
> The Cooks,
> Beautiful Goddesses of Hospitality!"

Mommi's and Aunt Syl's faces were radiant.

"Norman, I see you still spout that atheist Communist talk," commented Godfather.

"When's the last time you been inside a church, Pops?" answered Norman as he tucked his napkin in front of him.

"I stay out of 'em because I believe in Jehovah, not because I don't."

"No religion or politics at the table," commanded Mommi.

We were all seated at the table, and as usual I was sitting next to Teddie. I was anxious to appear sophisticated in Norman's eyes.

Our first course was a pungent, light broth to whet our appetites. As we began to eat, somehow my left arm heading mouthward with a spoon full of soup snagged on Teddie's right arm, which was headed toward her mouth. My left hand caught the edge of Teddie's bowl, dumping hot soup into her lap and spashing some over onto me.

"I told you to use your regular hand," Mommi bellowed, as she jumped up. Aunt Syl buzzed around trying to clean Teddie up while muttering, "A left-handed female is a bad sign they say. Handmaiden of the Devil. Winnie, make her use her right."

"She knows better than to eat with her left hand," Mommi apologized to Norman.

Nauseous humiliation made me weak.

Then Norman, with great flourish, took his soup spoon in his left hand and very slowly ate his broth. Then Stella, following his lead, picked up her spoon with her left hand and did the same thing.

A hush fell on the table as he finished, wiped his thick mustache and said, "I taught myself to use my left hand, because it was . . . well, different. I also paint with my left hand. The problem was not her left hand but that Teddie was sitting too close to her, practically in her lap, so no wonder there was an accident."

The conversations resumed.

"I wonder what number came out. I don't know 'cause the cops busted Baby again," said Mommi, finally serving her own plate.

"Call Sol. I bet he can get her out in no time," Norman suggested.

Baby was our lemon-yellow numbers runner with a wide gleaming lispstick smile that revealed a gleaming gold front tooth with a diamond imbedded in it. Baby worked hard. She went from house to house, climbing up six flights of stairs, running down fire escapes and crossing rooftops as she fled the "bulls" when her banker did not pay them off. It was just a ritual that her numbers banker, the cops, and Baby performed often when she was arrested, fined, and thrown in jail for a few hours and then released.

Unfailingly she would return and sit down at our kitchen table, unbutton her blouse, lift up her parachute size bosoms and release yards of long number sheets that unfurled to the floor, and silently scribble the day's digits. Everybody played the numbers in Harlem. They went to funerals of strangers to get the numbers on the caskets. They purchased *The Daily Mirror* to decipher what number the cartoon *Ching Chow* prophesied through his body language. They went to sleep in order to dream a number. Folks who had no formal education composed complex algebraic formulas and numerical charts with the help of dream books that gave detailed history of past numbers and foretold future ones.

"Pass the ri . . ."

"Her banker must have forgotten to cross someone's palms," said Daddy.

"Call Solomon Lewis, the big-time cop," repeated Norman.

"He's a detective, not a cop," said Godfather, "or a grown man drawing pictures."

"These biscuits are light as . . ."

"Do you have chestnuts in the stuff . . ."

"So, tell me. Do you want to attend the Town Hall rally with us?" asked Stella.

"Oh yes, I would love to," I said, looking at Mommi.

"No. She can't. Pass the salt."

"Why? There are lots of high school students working with us. This would be educational, good experience for her."

"No. She can't. I need her home right after school."

"Please, please," I begged her in front of company, hoping it would embarrass her.

"Never mind," said Norman suddenly. " I bet you you never had your picture painted?"

"No," I said, fighting back bitter tears.

"All right then. Since you won't allow her to travel downtown to Town Hall to the rally, at least let her come to my studio. It's nearby, right on 125th."

"No. She can't. I have to keep a tight rein on that one. Bad blood."

"I want to paint her picture."

"For what? No! She has chores to do after school instead of wasting time. The devil finds work for idle hands."

"This is work. I'll pay her a model's fee."

"Model? Absolutely not!"

"I want her face. There'll be no men sitting around drawing naked women, I promise. Please let her come. It will be her first job. I'll pay her a regular model's fee."

"Why not?" Norman asked, holding Mommi prisoner with his eyes, "She's perfect for what I want to capture."

"I don't know about this art foolishness."

"Think of it as a gamble. One day then you'll have two of my paintings that may be worth a lot of money. And she'll be working."

"Welllllll I dunno."

⟞

It worked. I was allowed to model for Norman as long as I promised to turn over whatever he paid me to Mrs Feral in order to begin to pay her back for all she'd done for me all these years May Anna left me with her without a peep to see if I had a morsel to chew or a pot to piss. I promised. His studio was the entire top floor of a loft building on 125th Street and Seventh Avenue with miles of open space and a tiny room with a sink and a toilet. Large, pivoting windows set into the roof with linen blinds allowed him to have whatever light he wanted from any angle. Drying canvases were everywhere, leaning against the wall in long racks in his numerous easels, spread on the gray concrete floor along with splashed palettes, jars of water and paint brushes.

I was so excited my spine was buzzing. I knew that this was another one of those occasions in my life where my consciousness would lurch forward, and I would be forever changed.

Lately, since my fourteenth birthday, those moments happened to me quite a lot, fleeting seconds with lasting impact, that seemed to arrange my very cells, like the first time a man lurking an alley unzipped his fly and trapped my eye in fear, involuntary lust and shame, or the first time I saw a living thing die, when I watched an injured cat die inch by inch.

Looking at all the paintings actually made me light-headed from the falling volcanic bursts of color. They were paintings of worlds beyond flesh or geography. This sure beat Miss Lassitoe's stupid art class where the color brown was banned and she made us use orange to represent any brown-complexioned person. Everywhere there were comets of indigo darkness ascending to brilliant carmines and vermilions. His paintings were games with light and shade, here darts of light falling, there lozenges of light through a murkish haze, light rolling on water or glancing off cliffs. Then there were shifting streams and islands of color, which on closer look revealed minute embroidered figures, half faces, green with heavy-lidded yellow eyes, black with red eyes, pink with silver eyes, crowds of barely discernable figures overlaid with fragments of rectangles, strange eyes and noses of almost recognizable faces that doubled as profile and shadow masks. Lines and circles that revealed hidden shape and form; tiny images that caught my eyes and then slowly disappeared as I was looking at them, as they became smaller almost beyond the seeing. And on every canvas the sweep and swing of his brush was the motion of light and music and color in the air!

"It's magic," I said to Lewis. "Everything's moving, going somewhere. Everywhere I look the shapes fold into something new, growing like magic underneath my eyes!"

"That's what painting is. Magic."

"But is that right? Is that what I'm supposed to see?"

"There are no rules, you can only see what you can see."

"But is that what you mean when you paint?"

"I only mean what you can see and feel."

"Oh," I said, suddenly feeling awkward and shy under Norman's relentless gaze.

"Here, sit in this chair. I want to see you in the afternoon light," he said, pointing to a velvet armchair next to an easel.

"Tell me about the rally," I said, sinking down, stretching my legs before me and suddenly self-conscious of my white buck shoes and socks and pink fake leather jacket which was the current teenage style. "It was hardly mentioned in the newspapers."

"Are you surprised?" he asked, not taking his eyes off me.

"Did you and Stella go?" I asked, wishing I didn't look so girlish.

"Naturally, we are active members of the National Committee to Free the Rosenbergs. At least twenty-five thousand people from all over were at Carnegie Hall. Folksingers, Robeson, old, middle-aged, aware young people from all over, your age and younger, it was quite a showing."

"Did the little boys come?" I asked thinking of the faces of the three- and seven-year-old Rosenberg boys, their hair parted on the side, smiling trustingly out at the world.

"No," said Norman. "Our Committee is sworn to protect them as much as possible. What they are doing to their parents is anti-semitism, anti-socialist, and a crime against all progressive people in America."

"I wanted to go," I blurted out. "She doesn't let me do anything or go anywhere. I WANTED TO BUT YOU KNOW I CAN'T DO ANYTHING. SHE DOESN'T LET ME. EVERYONE AT SCHOOL MAKES FUN OF ME. EVERYONE KNOWS HOW STRICT SHE IS WITH ME. AS IF I'M SOME KIND OF CRIMINAL WAITING TO HAPPEN. I HATE HER!" I shouted, and then broke down. I cried for Ethel and Julius, for their two little boys, and for anyone else I had heard of who ever suffered injustice.

Under his skylight the light paled and and grayed into dusk. I wrapped myself in the comforting soft gloaming and thick silence and knew that words were unnecessary between us.

Then he rose suddenly and said, "It's late. You're still a school-girl and I'm a painter with pictures to paint. Are you okay?"

"Yes, I guess. When are you going to start painting me?"

"Oh, I started to do that the moment I saw you. I'll be finished soon."

—

With my books under my arm, I ran from Jr. High School 81 on 120th Street and 7th Avenue to 125th Street. As I quickly passed by I tried not to hear the loud, jazz organ music that flowed from bars whose windows I was not even allowed to look in, the Baby Grand, the Braddock Bar, the Club Shalimar, the 125 Club. Why was there so much jazz organ played in Harlem? Could it be that syncopated organ peals reminded folks of church?

Norman's studio was across the street next to a black bookstore, "The House of Common Sense and Proper Propaganda." As I reached the top flight I could hear excited voices coming from his loft. Lewis's voice rose above the others.

". . . the dilemma . . . the trickbag . . . of black artists . . . development of the artist is being hammered by a desire . . ." he glanced in my direction and continued, "obligation to make political art while political commitment, in my opinion, automatically compromises aesthetics."

Eight men and two women were seated at a table. Some faces I recognized from Lewis' class. I didn't dare enter into the center of things but hung around the edges near the storage bin, listening with every cell, memorizing their faces as they spoke and trying to comprehend, trying to learn. I didn't understand a thing they were talking about, but I vowed that someday soon I would.

"Is it true that the artists should work from the particular to the general?" asked a thin, restless woman with light eyes who I knew was a sculptress. "Or is it the other way around?"

"Art is NOT architecture!" pronounced a round, red-faced, bearded man as he pounded his pipe on the table.

"This is the fifties, not the twenties, no more passé social realism for me," exclaimed an intense, skinny young man with a goatee and a beret. He was the image of the proverbial painter as he jabbed his long thin fingers in the air.

"No more painting with a subject. Naturalism ain't nat'chl and realism ain't real and it don't mean a thing if it ain't got that swing," he laughed at his own humor.

"But Ernie," objected a tall, dark man who later was to become famous for his biblical-like heroically proportioned figures of uncompromising strength, "no pictures without a theme. "

"Social realism, ghetto art, " sneered the other woman in the room.

"But," Norman asked as he motioned to me to come closer, "we cannot afford to say that great art must rise above racialism."

I tiptoed closer and took a seat as the sculptress challenged, "Why?"

"Because," Norman sighed exasperatedly as if explaining to a small child, "Black artists have a powerful enemy with which to contend in the superiority complex of the white—"

"You want both things," the sculptress said, her voice rising angrily, "you want to be abstract, you want to be realistic, at the same time you want to be racial in your art and yet universal."

"You're right," answered Norman, "I am all those things and much more. I used to paint our struggle. But the folks that I wanted to look at my pictures didn't so I became involved in unions and mass demonstrations—that's what reaches them. Painting doesn't. Everybody wants to dictate to the black artist. Black folks want him to paint their story. White folks want him to paint their version of our story.

"The struggle for the black artist in America is to find his individual soul. It takes courage to break out of the propaganda mold black and white have made for us. Here is proof," he said waving a copy of *Art News*. "This old fart of a critic says that, and I quote, 'Norman's paintings are too lovely to be important.' That's only because I'm not painting the white view of black life. It takes courage for a black artist to distill and soften an individual vision of beauty." As the rest cheered him, Norman joked, "That's my manifesto for today."

They resumed discussing painting, the materials they used, their various methods of operation, their visions, how many drafts they made or the story behind a work of art, until the light streaming through the skylight turned dark.

Suddenly, Norman turned to me, saying, "Friends, observe my young silent friend over there. She lives in a very American family where a grown man who 'draws' is considered an idler. In her junior high school, right here in Harlem, only the 'slow' kids are encouraged to draw and furthermore (are you ready for this?), whenever a student depicts Negroes in a drawing the color brown cannot be used. Orange instead of brown must be used for Negro flesh tones! Right here in Harlem!"

Later when Norman escorted me down the stairs he said, "I hope you aren't disappointed. But I wanted you to hear how artists talk. I wanted you to begin to understand that art is intellectual as well as emotional and physical. I thought you might enjoy it."

"I did," I said, too full of all that I had seen and heard to talk.

"You did? What did you learn today?"

"Last week I learned how to look. This week I learned how to listen."

"Good. My portrait of you is almost finished. Come back next week."

—

"So tell me about Racine and Molière," Norman said, as if continuing an ongoing conversation as I walked into his studio the next week. He was sitting at his easel.

I had been waiting for him. "*Tartuffe* I like because I know all about religious hypocrites. And Phaedre fell in love with her stepson. I . . . I"

"Go on . . . continue," he said, his eyes looking from me to the canvas as he wielded his brush.

"It got me started reading plays. I read this play about some people on a ship but they didn't know that they were dead. *Outward Bound* is the name and I just finished a book about 116th Street," I answered as I watched him dip his brush in various colors and spread them on his canvas in varying tones and shapes.

"*The Street.* You read that in school?"

"Oh no, Mrs. Hutson at Countee Cullen Library showed it to me. I liked it better than *Native Son.*"

"Why?" Norman kept the conversation going as he painted a little, stopped, studied me intensely, and then returned to his work.

"Because I pass by 116th every day. I know the stores Lutie hates to shop in. I see her son Bub with a key around his neck and every apartment building has a nasty, crazy ole Super living in the basement. I know *we* do."

Norman laughed but I couldn't tell what that meant. He was a complicated man, sharp, pointed, bittersweet and with a dry sense of humor. He continued to work without comment. Sunlight glimmered against the skylight. I listened to the sighs of his rapid brushstokes.

"But you know my favorite book of all time?"

"*The Bible?*" he laughed, his huge eyes brimming with humor.

"*Black Thunder.* About the slave revolt in South Carolina. About Gabriel Prosser. I wish they would make a movie."

"I know what part you'd want to play."

"Me too."

"JUBA!" he and I yelled at the same time.

"Bontemps wrote it in thirty-six. The year I was born and I'm just reading it. Mrs. Hutson showed me that one also."

"Go on, what else?"

"Yerby, *The Foxes of Harrow.*"

"Did you like it?"

"Loved it. Especially the love parts. Duels and voodoo and Quadroon mistresses. And the best thing was that you didn't even know the author was colored."

"What else?"

"The latest issue of *Wonder Woman* and I reread all of my *Grimm's Fairy Tales.*"

"Hmmmmm. I like that. Comic books and fairy tales give the truest picture of life," he said as he swirled more paint onto his canvas.

"In what way?"

"Because in comic books and fairy tales you can see the magic that is at work in our lives."

Underneath Norman's brush, crowds of microscopic figures were taking shape, wriggling free from its imprisoning swabs of color.

"What about your real mother?"

The swish of his brush strokes thundered in my ear. Billions of particles streamed back and forth in a jagged diagonal of sunlight streaming through the skylight. A mosquito looped around and fell dead.

"What about her?" I asked angrily.

"Who is she?"

"I'm illegitimate. My mother left me," I finally murmured.

Only when his paintbrush made a hollow clatter on the floor did I realize I had spoken aloud. Lewis turned and looked at me, his face a huge globe of rock with no light, then he looked away before he looked at me once more.

I waited in the thick silence, scared, shamed, and angry at everybody, especially at him. When he spoke, his voice seemed to come from someplace other than his throat.

"You're not too young to realize that no life is illegal, illegitimate." Like a moon going through its phases, his face was slowly becoming full of light. "You are a recurring child. Like Jesus. There's an old folk belief that there is only one child born to one single mother. The same child reoccurs down through the ages to teach humanity a lesson."

"What lesson?" I asked, totally fascinated.

"Who knows? But look at Jesus, Mary, and Joseph. There's gotta be some lessons earned from that little trio. Even if it's just that all God's chillun got ancestors, including you. Ancestors fill a place no mother or father can. Living parents are not always able to live up to their responsibilities. Ancestors will watch over you always."

I had moved closer to him. We were eye to eye, in each other's orbit, feeling each other's pull, absorbing one another's light.

Suddenly his face became carved with deep grooves that were like the ones on the African mask sitting on his easel. "Now are you ready to tell me about the beatings?"

"What are you talking about?"

"What do you call these? he asked, grabbing my mashed up fingernails.

"Beatings are the most severe, the ones with the iron cord and the metal part cuts into my flesh, and when I protect my face I get these."

"Go on," he said, still not looking at me.

"She almost paralyzed me when the metal struck my tail bone."

"Go on," he said in a dry, strangled voice.

"Everybody laughs because whenever she comes near me, I always duck. I never know when she will pick up whatever is near her or slap me when she can catch me off guard with her thick, fat, ugly hands."

Norman was silent for a long time. The only sound in his loft was the swish swish of his brush against the canvas.

"I'm taller than she is now and I'm stronger. I could beat her. I ache to smash her. When she attacks me my hands automatically ball up into fists but I know I'll be damned to hell for thinking about hitting my mother. Because that's who she is. I have no other. When she sees my balled up fists she goes crazy on me with the iron cord. Everything about me just makes her mad. I hate May Anna for leaving me here with her. And what about my father? Where is he? I hate him too. Everybody just stands around and lets her beat me. Everybody's afraid of Mommi. She's so good.

She's so kind. I'm so lucky. Yet everybody inside and outside the house knows. The neighbors laugh when they hear me screaming. Nobody does anything. I'm tired of her beatings, her punishments, her insults."

And then to my own surprise and completely involuntarily, I started laughing as if I had just told a very funny joke. It must be my period, I thought, careening from one emotion to the next, wanting to laugh and cry at the same time.

Norman finally put his brush down and looked at me.

"My father whipped me just so I wouldn't forget what was waiting for me if I thought about stepping out of line. I don't remember what I did, but I do remember the cat o' nine tails. I remember the nine hard, brown, leather whips, the nine knotted cords. I do remember my terror, my pain, and my fury. In many black families there is no such thing as 'child abuse.' I'm not one of those black folks who sit around laughing about the violence and rigidity he endured as a child and then call it good home training."

"Why, Norman, why do we act that way?

"Oh, because beatings are in our slave past, our present lives are still so harsh, and we have a lot of rancid, misdirected anger."

"What can I do?"

"Stay there till you finish high school. Leave the next day."

"That's three more years."

"You'll make it."

"Once when I was younger, a social worker wanted me to go to another home. Now I have no choice."

"Here," he said. "Today I want to give you a palm tree, a poem, and a painting," he said, handing me a small white box. "This is for you."

I opened it and it was a dazzling gold palm tree lying on a piece of parchment with graceful script written in purple ink. I recognized it as the same hand that signed Norman's paintings.

She does not know
her beauty
She thinks her brown body
Has no glory.

If she could dance
Naked
Under palm trees
And see her image in the river
She would know.

But there are no palm trees
On the street
And dish water gives back
no images.

—William Waring Cuney

As soon as I finished, Norman took my hand and led me to a full length mirror. "Look at yourself," he commanded.

And I looked at my reflection, wishing that my skin was lighter, that my blouse would stay in my skirt, that my socks would not sink down into my loafers, that my hair was thin and straight and that my behind was smaller. Wishing that folks would think me beautiful. I turned away from the mirror.

"Isn't she beautiful?" Norman said. "Oh yes, some folk say that every part of you is 'illegitimate' and beyond the pale, if you'll pardon my pun. Your skin is the color of things dark and forbidden; the unruliness of your hair is legend; your big behind is unfashionable, your lips too thick, too full.

"But others say that Cassiopeia, a beautiful Queen of Ethopia, drove Venus mad with jealousy so Venus turned her into a star. But even in heaven, Cassiopeia was a diva and turned into a constellation of stars. And I hear that lots of women pay for lip and behind implantations and suntans."

I laughed, I couldn't help it. I was giddy from all the things I was feeling.

"Stand still," Norman commanded. "Don't ever turn away from your mirror. Look at yourself." I did and this time, in Norman's mirror, I was aware of my beauty and May Anna's presence. May Anna was in the color and kink of my unstraightened hair; she was in its springy curl. I felt the magic of hair that grew before birth and beyond the grave; I saw in my hair the power and strength of unknown ancestry.

"Exquisite. I would never try to duplicate your beauty. I can only hope to translate," said Norman as he finally revealed his painting.

A crimson bird rising from a pyre of ashes. My right eye emerging, almost timidly, from a misty rainbow of muted colors was a sunrise. Underneath the eye was a fragmented sparkling translucent raindrop. The left eye had a lurking familiarity to mine except that the iris was ongoing spirals of little people, crowds of humanity. On both cheeks were luminescent stars and crimson birds flying from a pyre of ashes drawn so small and intricate, at first glance they looked like freckles or moles. In the bottom right-hand corner, right above his signature in purple, were the words, "Girl Phoenix."

28

One Hundred and Twentieth Street and Lenox Avenue wasn't the only place in America where violence and morality were inseparable. Over the radio, Congressman Frank Wilson declared that "America is dealing with mad dogs who have no regards for morals, human life or decency. We must treat them accordingly. I urge that the atom bomb be dropped if it can be used efficiently. In my book, one American boy is worth all of Asia."

Representative Joe Smith condemned the famous Swedish actress with molten eyes shaded by lush, thick eyebrows, along with her Italian lover and their illegitimate son. "I want to read into the Congressional Record," he said on the Senate floor, "that Ingrid Bergman is a disgrace to American women. I'm glad she is a foreigner."

On the nation's front pages, a photo of the mystical smile that lit the wan face of the condemned mother of two boys was under a caption that chortled, Atom Bomb Spies to Burn in Electric Chair!

And in far-flung outposts on the planet the sun turned black from nuclear bomb tests while on 120th Street Rose's piano shrieked in hysterical, staccato high C, on the day before her wedding, as she struck the note again and again, sobbing, "Maybe I could get married by proxy like Ingrid and Roberto, maybe I could live my whole life by proxy, I don't want to get married," and then her piano gave a dissonant moan as she laid her cheek on its keys and cried. I sat next to her on the narrow piano bench and gingerly pulled the dirty Band-Aid off my latest bruise. It was a deep, bloody, jagged line cut into my flesh on the underside of my left arm near my elbow. Although it was already beginning to heal, there was purplish thick blood oozing out under the scabby surface that I sucked as I tried to console her.

"Don't get married," I said, chewing my scabs, "if you don't want to."

"Oh I don't want to get married, I don't want to get married, I don't want to get married!"

I looked at her and lifted my elbow to my mouth to suck the blood out of my wound. When I did that it seemed to ease the soreness.

"Stop that," said Rose. "You'll get an infection. Does it hurt?"

"A little," I said, not wanting to talk about it, "but why are you getting married if you don't want to? I thought you liked Cedric."

Rose laughed dryly and said, "Oh he's all right, he's 15 years older than I am and set in his ways."

As Rose reached for a package of Band-Aids she continued, "Want to hear what my future husband told me when I told him I needed to have my piano?"

"No."

"He said that if I had to I could practice in the church basement." After we both finished laughing she took my arm and examined it.

"What did you get it for this time?"

"Oh, you know. It was a This-and-That whipping. But it's really about Clarence. Claims we are talking about her. Plotting against her."

"How come she lets you go out with him?"

"His family is big in St. Martin's. His mother is President of the Altar Guild. People would talk."

"You'll need to put a Band-Aid on it so it won't get infected."

"Rose, you don't have to marry him . . . do you? I mean . . . You are not . . . are you?"

"No," Rose said.

"Then why?"

"Don't ask. I can't tell, Gin-gin, so don't ask me again."

I wondered, what was so awful that she couldn't tell me but was powerful enough to make her get married when she didn't want to?

"What about Cedric?" I asked, trying to come at it from another way.

"What about him?" she asked, banging a bass note with her left hand. "What does he want?" Rose asked, repeatedly striking the low note as if she were trying to behead it. "Money, food, sex, and money in that order."

"But do you love him?" I said after we finished laughing.

"That kind of question belongs in a movie. In real life, love is a man you can fall back on," Rose answered almost in the exact same timbre as her mother.

"Oh Rose," I moaned. "Your wings are clipped. Why do you need someone to fall back on if you are too frightened to fly?"

"Birds fly. Women eat and have babies and need a roof over their head and a steady man."

"What about your music?"

Rose stood up and shouted, "My music? Who do you think I am? Every well-bred Negro girl plays the piano and sings in the choir but we all don't get to be Phillipa Schuyler or Marian Anderson!"

"O Rose," I moaned again as I licked my wound and tasted my blood.

"Oh Rose, oh Rose, oh Rose, Oroseorose orose," she mimicked me angrily. And then she slammed down the ebony lid over her piano's black and white teeth.

"See, I hate discord. I am not like you. See, I hate fights. I hate it. I can't stand it. They make me nervous and nauseous and upset. I'm like the animals in the forest that scatter before a storm, but you think nothing of walking into a whirlwind.

"What are you talking about?"

"I'm almost twenty-one years old. Cedric wants to marry me. He told Mommi and showed her his bank book. He's got two thousand dollars saved up. Mommi is ecstatic."

"Then let her marry him," I said.

"Suppose we were all like you. Can you imagine what kind of world this would be if children spoke their minds and women did what they wanted to? You know what, Joan of Arc, I just like a little harmony in my life."

"I think you are weak, just an orthodox coward," I said, turning my back to leave.

"Shut your damn mouth," Rose cried after me. "At least I know how to avoid getting my ass whipped," she screamed, "that's one thing you never did know and you still don't!"

—

A stained-glass Virgin Mary smiled wanly, pale against a background of blood red and torrid blue, her hands raised slightly almost as if in a nonchalant blessing, her head and halo slightly tilted to her left shoulder as if straining to get a better view of the bridesmaids and their escorts, marching two by two down the wine carpeted aisle.

The wedding guests perched on their wooden pews in their finery and marveled at the splendor of the all-white wedding. Even the groom and his attendants wore white, and from that day Rose's wedding was always known as a trendsetter for Harlem wedding fashions.

However, no one paid attention to the bride's loud and persistent sobs. Everyone pretended that it was just nervousness and would soon end. But they grew louder, becoming angry and then pleading, and no one could mistake the language of her tears.

"No! No! No! I DON'T WANT TO BE A WIFE! I DON'T WANT TO BE A MOTHER!" I understood that everyone knew that Rose's crying was the only protest left to her and that they meant to squash her rebellion by ignoring her tears.

As she howled, the organ growled the beginning of Lohengrin's Bridal March, signaling that it was time for the march down the aisle. Rose's shrieks reached the rafters. Amid the clamorous organ and bride's loud laments, Father Broyard was tense and grim as all eyes focused on Rose. Encased in a heavy white veil and shimmering satin, Rose slumped on her father's arm, her shrill cries now diminished to a low drone. She took one step and then stood stock still. But Daddy kept marching in time to the music, dragging his daughter until she had to take another step to keep from falling. She made her way down the aisle, stumbling and sobbing. Seated near the aisle, I felt the blasts of grief that shook her body as she stumbled by. I could smell her perfume and her sorrow. Her pain hung in the air. Like a premonition it hovered and diffused and resurfaced everywhere, in the flickering candles, in the shapes cast by sunlight and shadow that landed on all surfaces.

I watched Daddy and Rose finally reach the side of the grim-faced groom. As they stood beside Cedric at the altar, the lights of the church were abruptly dimmed. There was a moment of hushed silence broken only by Rose's plaintive wail. Then a lyric soprano seated in the choir loft rose, and accompanied by the organ, sang "Because."

It was a popular wedding song, and the soloist was always an operatic female whose high voice teetered on the edge of human audibility. The lyrics spoke to the groom and told him that his voice caused roses to grow at his bride's feet and that God had led the bride to him through tears (which was certainly true) and joy. At this point in the lyrics the soloist always became agitated and geared up along with the music for the climax.

Until now, music and lyrics were sweetly serenading the groom. But at this point they changed and became feverish and shrill. Any hint of bass in the song was soon drowned by an impatient and shrill soprano. "I'll cherish thee through light and dark, through all time to be," the soloist promised. "Even eternity," she added as as she shrieked victoriously, "Because God made you mine." It was not a sweet love song, but a war chant, a declaration, full of the arrogance that only a human being who claimed God was on her side could possess. The wedding guests seemed busy inside themselves and rapt in the music. Rose sobbed through the entire song. The soloist finished and sat down.

Rose's sobs did not subside as she exchanged wedding vows. The ceremony was hastily performed, and underneath the joyful peals of the organ, Rose was being dragged up the aisle by her new husband, still sobbing. But now, her veil was thrown back, exposing her tear-sodden face. She did not seem to care, and the crowd followed behind her, offering congratulations.

When I emerged from the dim church into bright daylight I was surprised to find it was the same afternoon, so much had happened inside. Standing on the stairs of St. Martin's I saw Rose, still sobbing, enter a black limousine that immediately whisked her away to her wedding reception. But the bottom of her wedding dress was trapped in its doors and skimmed over the asphalt streets, fluttering in the wind, becoming crumpled, torn, and a dirty, wind-tossed white.

Kisses were in the air. Girls kissed each other on the lips, men hugged each other and pounded each other on the back, young boys kissed old ladies, teenagers French kissed in the dark as everyone at the wedding reception became part of his own fantasy. Mommi was Queen Mother Winnie in her lace powder-blue gown and hovered over the royal couple, while Daddy was gentle-voiced Spencer Tracy shyly accepting congratulations in *Father of the Bride*. At the wedding table, Aunt Syl lifted her champagne glass and crooned "Danny Boy" with a perfect Irish accent, while Teddie went from table to table saying "This is a big fête, eh?" in her clipped pseudo-Bermudian accent. The octogenarian band members played "Bewitched, Bothered and Bewildered" in quick tempo and imagined they were young, hot, and really jamming, while the music confused the wedding guests who couldn't tell if they should lindy hop, slow drag, mambo, or calypso, and so they formed a conga line and one, two, three, kicked the length and width of the dance floor. The band leader imagined he was Al Jolson as he crooned, "O how we danced on the night we were wed," as Cedric twirled and dipped his bride across the dance floor as he had once seen Gene Kelly spin Betty Hutton around in a movie whose title he couldn't remember. The reception hall was decorated with crepe paper, tinsel, and balloons in counterfeit colors of romantic fantasy.

And I was Cinderella, secretly waiting her turn, gazing at Rose as she laid her head at exactly the same angle that Anna Marie Alberghetti did on John Derek's shoulder in *Lost Horizons* before they escaped to Shangri-la for an endless honeymoon.

29

In the year Rose got married, poppies and foxes appeared in Harlem. From West 110th Street advancing to 120th Street and east to 125th Street on the south and 155th Street on the north, from Morningside Avenue, Seventh and Eighth Avenues, St. Nicholas Avenue, Madison Avenue, and Lenox Avenue, a pestilence of poppies raged in our streets. Every Sunday morning, on his way to his Holiness Temple Sanctuary of Spiritual Baptists, Daddy stuck a crepe-paper poppy, a reddish orange flower with scalloped edges and a bright green paper stem, in his striped lapel. But the poppies that caused the plague were real ones, crushed to a white powder, packaged in glassine envelopes and sold in candy stores, hallways, and on street corners. Everywhere I saw men (for at that time they seemed the most vunerable; they certainly were the most visible) rendered inert in public places, spit drooling from their flaccid lips, their nodding heads bobbing listlessly like broken flowers, on the drooping stems of bent backs, their bowed knees folding their curved bodies into human question marks.

It soon became apparent that there was a "a dope infestation uptown in Negro Harlem," according to the *Daily Mirror*. But then, officials turned deaf ears to cries for help and declared that the cure for Harlem's dope problem, like its unemployment, police brutality, and inferior schools, was in the hearts and minds of the victims.

In the fifties, the influx of heroin in Harlem was considered a local problem and it, like illegitimacy, was merely fodder for avant-garde humor.

"Up in Harlem," joked a popular Beatnik stand-up comedian, "folks have a white Christmas every time their connection comes."

"Up in Harlem," continued the comedian, "there are so few fathers visible that scientists believe the local femmes have discovered a new fertility method called immaculate conception."

In that year, I welcomed the divergent news that a fugitive fox was running amuck in Harlem streets. It had escaped from the Bronx Zoo and was last seen in Mount Morris Park, which had wonderful trees, rolling hills, and thick underbrush. Newspapers reported that a fox in the city was not as strange as it seemed. In 1945, one had been found under the stands in Yankee Stadium, and an intrepid specimen was once captured by the police in Fort Tryon Park.

But this was a Harlem fox and therefore took on mythological proportions. Although it was first reported to be a smallish red fox, almost undistinguishable from a small dog, in the mouths of Harlemites it became the mammoth beast of Revelations that signified the Last Days. Queen Mother Providence, a hoary seeress with two-inch rainbow fingernails, claimed that it was she that made the fox manifest and only she could take it away. She posted bills all over Harlem announcing that she would indeed send more unusual animals among our midst until "All Ethiopia's children join the African Revertion Society and become Saved, become Sanctified, become Wonderful."

Flinty old race men atop wooden platforms claimed that the fox was a warning to Pharoah to give the Abyssinian people their civil rights. Harlem outlaws quickly claimed Brother Fox as a mascot since the critter was a cagey animal, expert at hiding, sagacious and cunning, wary with sharp senses, and expert at maintaining itself in the city in spite of being hunted.

Furthermore, not many city dogs were a match for Our Fox in

a fight and even fewer could run him down. Those that could he somehow avoided and as far as cars were concerned, Our Fox seemed to learn the traffic regulations and stay out of danger as much as possible.

The initial news of the footloose Harlem Fox cleared the streets with only fools, reporters, and white naturalists remaining on them. But by the third day a Harlem fox hunting club was formed and its members, calling themselves the "Talley Hos!," could be seen riding atop white horses through Mount Morris Park in black britches, red hunting jackets with brass buttons, black suede hunting caps, and riding crops, intent on rousing our foxy intruder.

The *Amsterdam News* slyly reported that 546 was the number most dreambooks gave for foxes. All of this came to an abrupt halt when the wily fox, usually invisible and cautious, started nocturnal barking. It was mating season, and it was his nightly cries for a mate that caused him to be flushed out and killed. When the poor dead critter proved to be a female, the sages of Harlem muttered, "Isn't that just like a woman to die for love?"

30

The facade of Rose's wedding complete, things descended to normal at home.

With Rose and Daddy gone, Teddie and I clung to one another even more.

Many times, at night, with Teddie in the lower bunk, I lay in my top bunk, afraid, listening to Mommi and Aunt Syl in the kitchen. Aware that I was awake, they pretended to talk to one another.

"Two things I can't stand is a loose woman and her ungrateful bastard. Almost sixteen years and has that May Anna even peeped in here to see if her crippled crab needed a crutch?"

"Sixteen years and not a peep."

"Sixteen years I been carrying this cross. Virginia is my cross to bear."

"I know, Winnie, your cross to bear. Don't worry."

"I know that my Redeemer liveth."

"Just watch out she don't big belly us in front of the neighbors."

"I look for that with a torchlight didn't I? Serve me right for being so kind-hearted and foolish enough to take her in. One look at May Anna and I should have known. What else comes from an empty bag of coals but dust?"

"I know, Winnie. Guinea hen don't make ramgoat, that's for sure."

Pause.

"Years of caring for other folks' children and what do I have to show for it?"

"I know, Winnie. Sharper than a serpent's tooth is an ungrateful child."

"Now Sheltering Arms says I'm too old for new foster children. Think of all the different ones I could have boarded with the space she's been taking up all these years. I tell you, my kind heart cost me a lot."

"I know, Winnie, all these years and water's still more than flour."

"All these years and we still renting in Harlem. Everybody else is moving left and right to Long Island and we still here."

"I know, Winnie, remember how nice it used to be when we first arrived? No crime. No juvenile delinquents?"

Pause.

"I see those girls talking loud on the corner and letting boys paw all over them. Any body in this house doing that she better not come home and she better not go anyplace!"

Pause.

"Keep her away from the other juvenile delinquents she may meet outside of this house."

"Some folks whisper that I'm too strict but who is in the kitchen is who feel the heat I always say."

"Father Broyard agrees with me. He says to watch her every moment so that she won't turn bad with boys or dope. He says there should be more parents like me. He says that I shouldn't spare the rod but that I should be careful not to get myself in trouble with the authorities. Nowadays the authorities trying to say don't beat your children. Tis no better beef, no better barrel to me cause I'd rather sit in jail for killing her rather than let her bring down my name in shame!"

Pause.

"Did you see the story in the *Daily News* today? The one about the sixteen-year-old who had a baby in the toilet and her mother didn't even kn——"

"They should put her in the electric chair. Put hot coals up her and flog her in the streets." Then dropping all pretense of speaking to Aunt Syl she would scream at me, "SLUT! PROSTITUTE! DOPE ADDICT! TRASH! RUFFIAN! I know you are awake. You hear me? Before I let you shame me in public I'll kill you. If I can't beat you to death, I'll poison——"

"Winnie, please, don't upset yourself with that girl. You think people don't know how good, how kind you are."

"But I know some folks think my strictness is coldheartedness."

"I know, Winnie, but everybody know a thick husk hide sweet coconut milk, a cutting tongue veils a soft heart."

"And my slaps are love."

" I know, Winnie. Love."

The room would spin around at a dizzying speed in my head, propelled by their hissing voices. Sometimes I feared for my life.

———

I could hear her sobbing everywhere, in the rustle of the ailanthus tree that lived outside the window, in the whine of next door's vacuum cleaner, in the hoarse static of the radio, the blare and honk of car horns, a ringing telephone, an angry slamming door, in the clashing, clanging, banging sounds that rose from objects colliding on the concrete and banging and bumping on the asphalt only to resound in my lonely room.

"Shhhh, May Anna, please don't cry," I used to whisper to the sounds around me, "I don't believe a word she says about you."

"Why, why why why? Why is she so hateful and abusive to you?" May Anna asked as if I were the mother and she the child.

"Because," a voice from within me answered back, "because, May Anna, my invisible mother, you are in me."

May Anna would materialize in a line of light streaming from the small window, or in the crystal tear falling from the sunrise eye of Girl Phoenix. The folds and creases of clothes thrown carelessly on a chair would suddenly take on what I imagined to be her contours, the cracks and stains on the ceiling would rearrange themselves in what I imagined to be her face. It was a face that was my face that kept changing, a familiar face that I had never seen before, that wouldn't hold still. Fragments of cheekbones, eyes, lips, hair, and complexions rearranging themselves, flowing into one another, timeless flowing backward and foward with no boundaries.

Her crying fades and there is only the sound of the city streets, her faces break up, dissolve, diffuse, and become only light and shadow once more and I am alone in my room but she is in me. She is in me.

31

However, I could always depend on Clarence for affection. His full lips were always wet, his eyes full of humor and his hands never still. He was my first and only date, his family powerful enough so that Mommi dared not oppose him, he was my closest friend and yet I dared not confide in him. I was too ashamed of my background, while he was proud of his. An only child in a family of property owners and entrepreneurs, he was following the pattern of life they had cut out for him, and now that he had put in his time in high school, he was anxious to soldier in Korea. Then he would return home and get a Civil Service job, move to Queens, anxious to settle down after having seen the world.

I could not tell him how only through reading could I escape the anger I felt all the time or that I wanted to go to college more than anything because it meant that I could live in the world and not just on 120th Street and Lenox Avenue. Why should I be different? Girls simply did not talk that way. Success was making it through high school without getting "caught," a good job and an employed husband.

We could, however, bring each other to orgasm but Mrs. Feral's voice in my head was stronger than any lust and prevented me from going all the way. I was determined to prove her predictions false and not follow in May Anna's footsteps.

One evening, coming from my part time job at Lane's Department Store on 14th Street where I worked after school and Saturdays, I dreaded returning home and instead got off the Sixth Avenue subway at Fourth Street. I immediately found myself in the Paris of my mind. On the sidewalks to the left and right was a feast of art for my eyes to devour.

It was the first time I had been in that kind of atmosphere. Sure, uptown folks were always turning the sidewalk into a stage. Wasn't there the wino gentleman with a tattered derby and red satin suspenders and a tapping right foot who, with the attitude of a virtuoso in Carnegie Hall, beat half-filled glasses of water with silver spoons? On 125th Street, sidewalk hustlers who painted portraits on velvet were as plentiful as barbequed ribs. And there were always the honey-voiced boys in huddles on every corner harmonizing about love. But back in Harlem the old glass beater was merely an eccentric, the serenading boys thought to be singing juvenile delinquents, while here in Greenwich Village I could see that the same things we did uptown were given the heady name of "art."

I strolled from Washington Square Park to Abingdon Square through the old houses with steep slate roofs and chimney pots, shining brass knobs on wooden doors, small-paned windows, ironwork fences, and rear informal gardens. Meandering on the sinewy secret streets, I let them lead me into cafés and tried not to gawk at the bearded poets howling to the skies and strumming guitars. The black tights and close-cropped, unstraightened hair of black girls walking hand in hand with long-haired white boys excited me.

I had read about Baldwin and Himes and Wright sitting in Parisian cafés writing great novels. Could a black girl do the same in the fifties in Greenwich Village? Maybe I could starve in a garret here and paint or write. Or both. I wasn't sure which yet. Maybe . . . maybe . . . who kno——

"Nigger, get back to Harlem," a sweating swarthy beefy-faced man blared his foul words into my ear and jolted me back to reality.

I was standing on MacDougal and Sixth Avenue, in front of gray-steepled Our Lady of Pompeii Church, watching its annual street festival. Too frightened to be angry, I backed away from the hatred in his eyes and headed for the train uptown. I returned to Harlem, telling myself it was only a temporary retreat.

Back uptown, Clarence told me that I had no business wandering around in Greenwich Village. "That oughtta teach you to stay in Harlem where it's safe. What were you doing roaming around among those weird freaks down there anyhow?" he asked when I recounted my adventure.

We were sitting on the steps of his parents' brownstone, looking out into the familiar streets. Our faces were no different from any other face. We all looked the same. The curses of the men, the moans of the women, the chanting of the playing children were noises as familiar to me as the pulse in my blood. The afternoon sunlight was right on time, zigzagging across the Harlemscape, dividing the buildings half in shadow, half in sunlight as it always did this time of year at this very same hour of the day. The naked woman who usually leaned out of a top-floor window, pretending ignorance of the display of her mountainous breasts, leaned out. As usual, the children playing in the street looked up at her window and snickered. The conk-head men and bleach-skin women, people who were locked out, clamoring to be included, deadlocked with each other for the merely ordinary satisfactions, passed by and were the same ones I saw yesterday and would see tomorrow.

"Don't you ever want to see anything different? I do. I want to go someplace far away from here," I said, irritated by his placid demeanor.

"You're almost eighteen, soon you'll be working and out on your own, then you and I can really boogie," he grinned, grabbing my hand and ignoring my question.

"But you'll be in the army then," pulling my hand from his.

"Probably Korea," he said eagerly, reaching for my hand again.

I stood up and faced him. His bespectacled eyes and calm face were puzzled. I was inexplicably overwhelmed by the ordinariness of it all.

"Clarence, don't you want to do something, go someplace?"

" I am," he said. "I'm going to Korea."

"Do you know about what's going on in this country? Places we can't eat and work at."

"Name one," he said, getting angry.

I was excitedly counting off on my fingers, "The Stork Club, Schrafft's Restaurant, the Telephone Company, I can't be an airline stewardess, and I can't walk around in the Village."

"Girl, what is wrong with you? What are you talking about? You just need to come over here and you know what," he half-joked and abruptly stood up as if to end the conversation. "You are a girl so why think about such things?"

Why was I indeed when I knew I could not bear to lose him, I asked myself as I moved closer to him.

Our gropings were a dangerous game of brinkmanship but I knew no matter how close we came to the edge Clarence would never force me. I trusted him.

"Mrs. Feral paid a visit to my mother yesterday," he said looking down.

"What?!! Why? What happened, what did she say? Why didn't you say something before, wha——"

"They talked so I couldn't hear. But afterwards my mother told me that Mrs. Feral was a good Christian foster mother and they both felt that you were a bad influence on me."

"And what did you say?"

"What could I say? I tried to tell her that you got a lot of whippings."

"What did your mother say?"

She said, "What is Virginia doing to deserve them?"

And I, right there in public, on his front steps, in full view of everyone, I screamed my life's story in the language of sobs. Clarence held me in his arms, kissed me and made soothing noises. He even made funny faces at me in an attempt to make me laugh and stop weeping.

"Clarence, come inside at once. I want to talk to you," his mother called.

"Yes m'am," he said quickly, turning away from me without a backward glance. "I'll be right there."

32

Fidel Castro had just attacked the Moncado Barricade de Santiago de Cuba. Lillian Helman said she wasn't a Communist and refused to tell who was, and after a long battle with New York City, the Savoy Ballroom was scheduled to close any day.

In my room the saccharine strains of Martin Block's "Make Believe Ballroom" floated from the wooden, cloth-covered Delco radio. Then the nasal baritone of Vaughn Monroe was followed by the melancholy wail of Frankie Laine's "That Lucky Old Sun." After his station break, the usually placid Martin Block spewed forth a diatribe on the vulgar music glutting up the airways and promised his listeners not to ever pollute their ears with Rock and Roll.

"Virginia, get in here, at once." I had been called like that before but why at the sound of her voice, this time, for no logical reason did the cosmos shift; why in that second did the world turn under my feet, the earth become skewed, slip a little as I felt the planet revolving and with it a sickening lurching forward of my life?

I followed fate and warily traced the sound of her voice entering the living room where Mommi was seated on the couch. Her brown eyes were glittering berries and I sniffed the room for her mood as Mrs. Feral picked up a square envelope on the coffee table and held it out to me. I took it, standing as far away from her as possible, trying to avoid one of her up-close flash backhand slaps in my face. I studied the enevelope, all the time keeping my distance and one eye on her. Inside was a white card. It was a block of cement, a stiff, unyielding white square piece of cardboard, an empty weak thin white with no casts or undertones. While I stared at it, from somewhere a thick charcoal smell of fire-escape barbecue coagulated in the air. A man in the window directly across from me leaned out the window holding up three fingers to a woman in the street below to indicate the last digit to come out. A yipping dog only punctuated the whirring sound in my head as I held the wedding invitation and caught a whiff of jasmine.

The raised black script curled around the darkening day's contours. The setting sun became a terrible blood red as I tried to stop the rush of letters pouring through my eyes.

theweddingofCoralandClarence
theweddingofCoralandClarence
theweddingofCoralandClarence

In slow motion, I watched the woman's heavy arm arc the air. Her upper arm quivered with rage, her pudgy fingers spread fan-like began to curl up one by one into a tight brown fist like a ball that grazed my nose and smashed my upper lip.

I smiled at her as if she had given me a caress. My eyes fixed on a falling white dot as disembodied voices floated above.

"Spoiled goods"

A pearl lay next to my bare toes, a pinpoint of irridescent lustre.

"Sneaking around in that car of his like the tramp you are."

A pearl is a tear drop, is one, crystallized tear.

"Marrying . . . nice girl. He told his mother he didn't know what kind of . . . you are. Well after I got through telling her . . . she was as worried as I was that you . . . pregnant . . ."

What is the journey of a pearl? Found on the bed of the ocean. Bought and sold. Passed through many hands.

You a virgin? Ha! You better be. I'm gonna have you examined and you mark my words it better be it better be up there it better be up there it better! yelled her voice from some far-away abyss.

It wasn't till later, alone in my room, when the feel of snot and blood and a shock of cold air on my naked gum made me realize that the pearl laying on the floor was my very own front tooth.

Hurt and then hurt.

I wrestle with my doubt

and flailing sorrow.

—Angela Jackson,
"The House of the Spider"

33

I only appeared to occupy my body when I was taken to the doctor. Mrs. LeNoire and Mommi warned me that if I didn't submit to this medical examination, I could be declared an incorrigible and sent into a home for wayward girls because it was still a few months until I was eighteen and on my own. Mommi added if I was not a virgin I would have to go there anyway because she was not running a whorehouse.

"When was your last intercourse, young lady? Really? We'll soon see if that's so lass. Roll up your sleeves, let's have a look at those arms. Now tell the truth and shame the divil you're not a virgin. True lass? You don't say? To be sure? But you do smoke the reefers young lass, don't you now? You're an innocent lass aren't you? Surely you can't be that good. My, we certainly are angry, aren't we?"

"Yes," I sneered, "I certainly are."

We were at Sheltering Arms Children's Service with the one and same doctor I had seen for the past seventeen years.

Thus, continuing my intimacy with the state in the form of Dr. Regan and in the presence of Mommi and my social worker, Mrs. LeNoire, I followed his instructions to undress and lie down on the examining table. Although neither made any eye contact with me, the doctor and nurse both let me know silently that I was indeed disagreeable to them. Once I was on the table, the nurse became upset because I hadn't spread my legs and put my feet in the two metal stirrups. Irritably she did it herself, and carelessly covered my naked body with a sheet.

"You'll have to relax so I can examine you," said the aged doctor, exasperated at my locked muscles, as he unsuccessfuly tried to insert a cold, hard speculum in my vagina. He stroked my thighs as if to soothe a quavering cow as he once again pried them open. But the worst was when the doctor put on a rubber glove and thrust his finger inside of me, prying, poking and pressing again and again.

The hoary doctor's fingers probed and kept tapping against a membrane repeatedly as if he couldn't believe it was there.

"Ow," I said. " That hurts."

"You should have thought about that before. Be still." Dr. Regan answered. He withdrew for a few seconds only to start poking and probing, smiling to himself, enjoying some private joke as if he was alone. Lying there, flat on my back, against my will, my feet in metal stirrups, my thighs splayed wide open so that a doctor could verify my virginity in order to determine whether I would be sent away, was, I knew, my first rape.

"All's well, completely normal, she's intact," the old man reassured my foster mother and the social worker. He turned to Mommi and beamed.

"You have done a fine job, Mother."

I planned my revenge.

34

Blind, visceral revenge. Against everyone. Nothing less could assuage my pain. He was all I had in the world and I lost him. My only friend against all the others and I lost him. And my loss was public, for everyone was going to Clarence and Coral's wedding.

"Ya got a money maker between those legs!" the lounging men on Lenox Avenue use to shout as I passed through the gauntlet their eyes formed, but now I knew that the whole society was in agreement with them; the cave between my legs was the essence of my being, my one valuable part. Clarence wanted only that part of me; my foster mother had used it as a cudgel against my spirit; the State could poke and probe it, in order to ascertain whether the entrance had been broken into; if it had I would be criminalized and institutionalized. That dark hole was my only value in the world and therefore it would become my weapon for revenge.

With Clarence I revealed those parts of me that otherwise remained hidden. In my unintentional gestures, my impulsive word, my silences that never lied, I told him. Too embarassed to speak out loud, there were no omissions, only suppressions, no untruths, only masking, no hiding, only pretense. I spoke in a language I thought that made it clear that without him I could not endure my life, without him I would be an open, bleeding, infected wound.

Every day, several times a day, I walked up and down the street in front of his house hoping to catch sight of him. I didn't know what I would say or do, but wanted just the sight of him. I never saw him again; were he and his blue Mercury wiped off the planet? Had Clarence only existed in my imagination?

Mrs. Feral, on the other hand, was quite pleasant those days. After all, I would graduate from George Washington High School in June, start work downtown at Equitable Life Assurance Company as one of its first Negro clerks. She considered it a tribute to her discipline and high standards that I was a virgin after all. Now, she said, all I had to do was to work and bring home my paycheck to pay her back for all she had done for me. She left gifts around for me and told me I could have them if I wanted: a box of round green perfumed Myurugia soap individually wrapped in black and red tissue paper; a multicolored scarf with a map of the island of Bermuda on it; a cameo of a pale white woman with a long slender neck and upswept hair against an ebony background; a 45 r.p.m. of the Orioles singing "Just A Kiss And A Rose."

"Stay here," she coaxed. "You have no idea how cold and cruel the world is to a woman by herself. Why pay a stranger rent?"

I ran my tongue in the space where my front false tooth used to be as I listened to her, thinking, So now I was a woman, was I? Okay. I would immerse myself in sex. I would begin by giving away immediately to the first man I could find, what Clarence had unsuccessfully pursued for two years. Then, in the most flamboyant public manner, I would publicly earn those names that easily fell from her lips about me and May Anna. I would be seen with a different man every night, cause scandal, and have people talk and whisper and laugh as I walked down the street. I would bring low her high head. It was only in sexual abandon could I strike back. I needed men, lots of men, and I knew just where to look.

35

Back at the Savoy Ballroom on its closing night I searched for him. In the muted light I slid from male to male until I settled on my prey. When the music started he streamed toward me, gliding and skimming on the cresting sound waves, eyes ablaze with the excitement of music. His swaying body floated on the surface of the music's rhythm as he stretched his arms toward me and I quickly filled the half circle they made.

We both snapped our heads from side to side in time with the music. I arched my back, quivering as the notes rolled up and down my vertebrae. He edged closer, bending a leg, tilting his body to one side like a lopsided tap dancer, then swiftly standing upright, he continued toward me still in time to the music in a stiff legged two-step as if he carried a great weight between his legs.

He stepped behind me, nuzzling his head on the nape of my neck while I rested my buttocks, somewhere between his chest and stomach as he curled around me.

Finally he and I faced each other. I smiled at him widely, confident. His dark brown face was made darker by his cream colored suit. On his feet were pointed-toe cream and black patent leather shoes embossed with half moons. He, like everyone else, was dressed in his Saturday night function finery. I wiggled my bare shoulders and my skirt rose and billowed as he twirled me again and again, pulled me toward him, then outward, around and around, up, down, across and along the sides of the huge dance floor in a ritualistic, elegant dance of confrontation and synchronization.

He and I danced in perfect unison, then broke apart, our fingers locked as we improvised our steps, taking solo turns. Each of us in our own worlds, all the time in step with one another with music our only conversation. The brass, reeds, piano, alto and tenor sax crescendoed in an orgiastic melodic whirpool in which every trembling body on the shivering dance floor was sucked into and caused our hands to rise in the air and sway like palms in a summer breeze in a symbolic gesture of praise and benediction.

Filled with vengeful lust I followed him into the electric night. The Harlem night sky was blue black, her streets full of bodies glowing and emitting sparks of energy into her darkness like fireflies. Nowhere else in the city did the air throb with energy like it did uptown, night or day. He pressed his thumb in the small of my back and I let my quarry gently guide me toward his room. A man on the corner with knowing, wine-soaked eyes looked at us and winked.

We stopped in front of a worn brownstone house on Hamilton Terrace shadowed by an ailanthus tree. An urban tree, shallowly rooted, it seemed to shake off city soot and dust and grew everywhere. Wherever its seed dropped it pushed through the concrete and glutted the city. Its long, skinny leaves did not hide its sinewy branches but only swayed and sighed to us in the thin purple night air. As if they had their own will, a reverse law of gravity pushed our legs onward, up the stairs we climbed, which led to his bed.

In his room, seated on his single bed, with a flat lumpy mattress, the dance music no longer between us, we were forced to face each other.

Suddenly awkward and hesitant without the music uniting us, he looked at me and said, "You're a good dancer, May Anna."

"I know. So I've been told."

"I got some women named 'May Anna' in my family. You remind me of them."

"How's that?"

"They big-legged country girls like you 'cept you a big-legged city girl." I remained silent and he continued probing.

"I haven't seen you around before . . . Kinda young . . . for a . . . are you a . . . sporting gal?"

"Yes, I'm new around here."

I turned my face away from him as he took my chin in his hands. He opened my mouth and placed his tongue in the gap left by my absent front tooth.

Still clothed, I spread my legs wide open for the second time in my life. This time it was not to let an old white man, long white hairs hanging from his quivering nostrils, holding a probing cold steel instrument with rubber-gloved fingers, poke around my vagina. Now, an ebony, long, thick, swollen penis flailed and ripped against my vagina, each thrust a slash against my enemies until finally after several reconnaissances it rendered Mrs. Feral, May Anna, and Clarence to their knees as it tore away my hymen and filled me with its milk. How was I to know that the grief of my past and the torment of my future would merge in this moment of carnal revenge?

I ignored the man laboring above me and instead thought about men. Where were they? Certainly not in my neighborhood. What was a man? From the men I had observed they made it difficult for me to believe that women and men were the same species. Most of the men who stayed around were like parasitic appendages attached to their women, permanently fused to their bodies, nothing but a pair of gonads; a steady supply of sperm but a poor companion.

Jolted back to the reality of the room by the grunting of the stranger above me, the thought came to me that if I were to suddenly rise up and cannibalize him, twist off his head while we were fucking and leisurely eat it, he would continue to rock his body against mine in a mindless fervor.

"Why didn't you tell me? Did I hurt you?" he asked in a sudden fit of tenderness when he realized my previous condition.

"Yes, it hurt, but I didn't feel it."

He laughed and said, "My little virgin."

"Not anymore. You just took care of that," I reminded him.

We practically had to lay on top of each other, the bed was so narrow. The white peeling paint over the black iron bars gave it a diseased look.

"Who are you?" he repeated.

He tried to get me to talk but I wouldn't, so he told me his name but it didn't matter; he didn't matter: he was only Clarence; he was only my ineffectual foster father; he was only the ghost who sired me; he was only all of the men who were supposed to be important in my life who were little more than illusions that I had either lost or never known.

I tried not to notice that his dark body was long and lithe and his hands graceful or the questioning tenderness in his eyes when he looked at me. I did not want to feel anything as he described how he was beaten in the Tombs last week for correcting a police officer who called him out of his name. I didn't care how hard he was studying for the Post Office exam or about his relatives in Chester, South Carolina, or that he hoped to buy his mother a house one day and when he was a small child he watched his father die and made up his mind he never would. Why did he insist on trying to let me know who he was? Pretending to absorb his words, I looked around his room; its sordidness was a perfect match for my mood; its worn shabbiness a perfect environment for my disaffected heart.

The intense, strange boy (for although he was older than I and legally adult we were both less than grown and knew it) turned to me. For the first time I noticed his finely chiseled nose and high cheekbones and intense dark eyes.

"Anthony," he had said. As if to make sure I heard him, he repeated, "My name is Anthony James Thomas. Just so you know, May Anna."

I enjoyed my secret vengeance and tore up my dance partner's telephone number.

36

The din of the courtroom ignited into loud sounds and movements. Above, a sonorous grandfather clock signaled the advent of noon. For the first time during our three-hour ordeal, the judge and his clerks looked directly at us. A court officer motioned that I should come forward as Mrs. Wallings cradled her arms to receive Kelvin. I couldn't move but frantically continued whispering in his ears. Words were dry in my mouth, for I was at the hardest part where I must tell him, quickly, without embroidery, that I conceived without wanting him and once hated the idea of him and now, because I really wanted his present and future to exceed what I could even imagine then, we had to separate. That I knew, without understanding the mysteries of life, that he was both mother and father lost and regained, lost found ancestor and descendent, rejoined and separated once again. When would our painful cycle stop?

37

The sticky Harlem summer diffused into a tingling leaf-blown spice-colored autumn. Thin summer dresses became hooded wool coats, and sandals with winking red toenails were exchanged for over-the-thigh, black shiny Russian boots as dread coursed through my bloodstream and ate at my nerve endings, made my saliva bitter, poisoned my tastebuds, made me sweat with terror and freeze with fear in the same moment.finally making me light-headed with fear. What a cosmic joke. Vengeance against Mommi was the force that would make her evil oracles about me come true.

I cajoled, I bargained. I pleaded with God. I went through my days in slow motion, becoming familiar with the weight of each second. Time was an endless saga of prayer. Surely it will come in the morning. In the morning I prayed for blood in the afternoon. Certainly by bedtime. Or again by the next morning.

Numb, I graduated from George Washington High School and started working downtown, and enrolled in my first college course at City College in the evening, all the while terrified and nauseous.

"Virginia, is that you?" a voice called after me one evening on the gray and white campus as I walked to class. "Virginia, it's me, Rose." I was glad for the sharp autumn chill, for the sweater I could hide under. Rose, who had taken to wearing only purple clothes, even down to her shoes, hugged me. She looked as if someone had turned out the lights in her eyes.

In the half-light of the lamposts on City College campus her purple hat and coat glowed. She carried a large purple purse with a huge purple flower.

"I'm on my way back to Queens, I just come over here to do some shopping for things I can't get back in Queens. I miss Harlem. I miss the old neighborhood. I got a promotion, now I am a GS-5. Cedric is slated for a permanent in the Post Office. Mommi's found us a one-family in St. Albans and you know what, it's not so bad being married to him. I don't miss my music half as much as I thought I would. Secretly, I did think that I would be another Phillippa Schuyler but that wasn't very practical. How foolish it was to waste those long hours sitting at the piano where nothing else mattered to me but the beauty of music, I hated it so."

"Don't cry, Rose."

She blew her nose and continued in small talk. Chattering away as I waited for her to ask me about Clarence and Coral. "What happened, Gin-gin, what happened?"

I was in such deep pain I couldn't talk about it even to Rose. "Nothing," I mumbled. "We had broken up before." Standing in front of the dark gray and white buildings, I wondered who was in more pain, Rose because she had married or me because I had not.

"Get out of there, Gin-gin. Soon. Get out. You finished high school. Go now." She laid a purple-gloved hand on my shoulders. "I had to get married because of her. Mommi begged me to get married. She didn't care who. Just as long as I had a big wedding."

"Wedding?"

"Yes, wedding. The white gown, the church, the respect and admiration of people watching her virgin daughter go down the aisle like a queen. It's all she wanted in the world and I was the only one could give it to her. She begged me. You should have seen her Gin-gin. My own mother on her knees begging me to grant her her only dream."

"I don't understand."

"They laughed at her when she was a young woman, they tied a tin can around her waist and chased her down the street and finally she was sent to another island, St. Kitts, I think, in an attempt to run away from the shame of what had happened to her in Bermuda. She was nine years old and she waited. Told her to wait until talk died down and they would sent for her. Finally after she and daddy married they came to America where they could reinvent their background."

"Aunt Syl hinted at something once but she never told me. Tell me."

"Mommi was bothered, that's what she called it. Bothered by a British Crown Lands superintendent who rode around on a fine government horse trying to sway poor country folks to resettle in the deepest sections of uninhabited lands where even the crudest roads quit. He had a reputation for who he was. His kind always loved Bermuda, Daddy said. Those were Daddy's exact words when he told me. Always liked a black woman and acted just like bulls let out of a pen. What happened to Mommi was a common, everyday thing, and it frightened Aunt Syl so badly that she had her womb taken out and never went near a man. Daddy grew up in the same parish with them. He saw it all."

"How did they all get together again?"

"Aunt Syl went looking for Mommi in St. Kitts after both her parents died. Daddy came a-courting Aunt Syl. They were all young. They all wanted to go to America. Daddy wanted, in his own way, to protect them since he had seen what happened. They all needed each other. He agreed to marry Mommi but it was Aunt Syl that he always loved."

"How did you find out?"

"Little by little. Through the years. Catching her in moments of relaxation. Eavesdropping on conversations between them.

Piecing all their tales together and some of my own inquiries. That sort of thing. I had to dig. You know how they are. Those people don't talk about the past. They won't tell you anything about themselves. Finally, Daddy told me before he left."

"Why did she beat me, Rose? Why did she hate me? She still does and I hate her."

"Don't, Virginia. She can't help the way she is. None of them can. Family. Blood. Class. That's just the way they are."

I couldn't answer. I just listened to Rose making excuses for something someone should have stopped a long time ago.

"She really thinks she's not doing you any harm. She did the best she could."

"She tells me the same thing, Rose," I said, removing her purple hand from my shoulders. "For eighteen years Mommi has been telling me, 'I'm doing the best I can.'"

38

If only I could be a hen that drinks it own eggs. I only half-heartedly tried to get rid of it because the sight of Helen lying in her casket with her arms around her dead baby haunted me. The one thing that I was sure of was even though I wanted the thing growing inside me to die, I wanted my own existence. Since I could not kill myself, it would succeed in getting born. Only then could I separate from this thing that had wormed its way into my womb like a thief. I would give it away, wanting nothing whatsoever to do with it. I did not want to see, smell, or touch it. Why, I asked, should I have to look at something that would come out of my loathsome body and look just like me?

It is before dawn. The taste of vomit is still in my mouth. She has been listening to me and as I close the bathroom door she emerges from the shadows. Although we are in our nightgowns, our last meeting is formal for it is a ritual we can no longer avoid.

"Open your blouse and let me see your breasts." Weary with nausea and despair, I obediently unbuttoned my blouse and took out my two swollen breasts tipped with engorged purple nipples for Mommi to inspect.

"Ahhhhhh," she involuntarily exhaled. The sound escaped from her again and again, causing her to deflate before my eyes, cracking her firm dark face into deep furrows of cascading torment.

In that moment I tasted my revenge. It was deep, thick, and sweet; bittersweet and fleeting for in that same moment I ached to kneel before her, to clutch her in a desperate hug and utter one word. *"Forgive."* Instead I caught the curled fist in midair and warned, "Don't you ever hit me again." Slowly, very slowly, the hand lowered. The fingers came unclenched one by one, the shoulders slumped and she shook her head.

"Whose is it anyhow?"

" Someone I met at a dance. I don't even know where he lives and I don't care."

"You did this on purpose didn't you, Virginia? "

"After all your predictions about me I thought your prophecies should come true. You wouldn't want to be a liar about me."

"Get out. Get out of my house right now." As I put my breasts in my night gown, slowly buttoned my blouse, I was already wondering, where would I go, who could I run to?

"Wait," said Mrs. Feral. "I have a way out of this mess. You can go away to a Home for Unwed Mothers. Then place the baby in my foster care. That way nobody has to know it's yours and I can still keep my head up. This way you can pay me back for all I've done for you. I'm too old to get any more foster children from the agency but if you . . ."

She must have known all along! Listening to her I know that she must have at least suspected and waited to confront me only after she had worked out her plan . . .

"Business as usual," I answered. "Just keep those monthly checks a-rolling in. And how many times a day will he get whipped? Four or five?"

"I whipped you in love."

"No! You whipped me in order to humiliate me. You whipped me because you hated me. You whipped me because you hated May Anna. You whipped me because I was a child and there was no one to stop you. You whipped me because you could."

"Is this the thanks I get for eighteen years of foster care? Eighteen

years I wiped your behind and cleaned your snot when your own
mother didn't want you, threw you away and never looked back,
and here you are you ungrateful wretch sitting on the river bed
talking the river bad!"

"I would never, ever let you get your hands on any child of
mine."

"You had good food in your belly and a clean place to sleep,
didn't you?"

"It was your job. You got paid for it. You were only doing your
job."

"Sharper than a serpent's tooth is an ungrateful child. If you
think that measly little state money covered all the times I worried
about you, think again. I was the idiot who watched over you for
eighteen years; I was the fool who tended you when you were sick
and didn't want you to die. I was the jackass who worried about
you growing up in Harlem and didn't want to see you on drugs or
in jail or pregnant like you are now. Good or bad, you had a family, you had a home, you had a mother, and like it or not, everytime you hear that word 'mother' it will be my face you see. Not
May Anna's face . . . but mine!"

"Whatever you gave me, I more than paid for. You took it out
of my behind! And before I let you raise a child of mine I would
rather burn it up in the incinerator!"

"Ungratefulness is worse than witchcraft! Leave this house, you
leave it with exactly what May Anna brought you with and nothing else!"

Mommi ran to her room and quickly returned with an ancient
battered, brown and yellow plaid cardboard suitcase with the
words written in a childish scrawl, North Carolina, Harlem, New
York. It was empty except for a carving wrapped in an old
chammy cloth, some whittled pine letters like leaves all spelling
L I V E. A faint aroma of tobacco clung to the musty chammy
cloth, discolored with age. I fingered them, trying to remember
where I had seen them before.

"Is that all?" I said to Mommi, to myself, to the universe. "Is that all," I repeated, unaware that I had spoken aloud.

"You think you came here with a treasure chest? Now you take your empty suitcase, let my door hit you where the sun don't shine but," she said, her face gleaming with tears, "mark my words, one day, I will step over you in the gutter!"

Although I was put out on the streets there was nothing unusual about the November day. The foggy air sagged with mist, overwhelmed by its own thick moisture. I passed the kiosk where I once traded comic books and glanced at shouting headlines screaming about a woman who refused to sit in the back of a bus in Georgia. All around me music rose from the sidewalks and endless gray skies yawned through the empty sockets of windowless buildings. The pervasive jazz seemed to limp in the air haltingly as if fatigued by its own fast tempo, yet a kinetic energy (even on a gray November day) throbbed in the air like a piano string vibrating from the memory of its own sound.

I walked the sidewalks that I had skipped back and forth to school on, still hearing the childhood rhyme, still unconsciously avoiding the cracks, not wanting to break my mother's back: sidewalks whose textures and patterns were tattooed on my heart.

As I maneuvered my way past flat eyes and ancient faces, lovers and cowards, crooks and cripples, three electric stabs of life jolted me and fixed me to the sidewalk. I stood still and listened. Three piercing jolts whose womb language was unmistakable. I. Am. Here.

Finally, at 116th Street I climbed down the subway stairs and paid my fifteen cents fare. The transition from sunlight to underground darkness was blinding but my eyes quickly adjusted and I saw a train already in the station, its doors wide open, waiting.

"One hundred sixteenth Street, last stop in Harlem," cried the conductor as I hurried through the turnstile, boarded the train.

39

In our family, Kelvin, men are needed. Husbands and fathers are loved but somehow they can't stay. Brothers are loved but they are jailed and murdered. We women give birth in a world where our sons and daughters have a better chance without us. I whispered to you my life, our history in that courtroom on our final day, sparing you nothing, and now I write it down believing that somewhere, somehow, you will read this and know that we are mother and son. Did a tomorrow without humiliation ever come for you? I hope so, else all this was in vain.

I placed you in Mrs. Walling's cradled arms and moved toward the judge's bench. Child, life is such a crapshoot, is there any greater act of faith in humanity then to give up a child to faceless strangers?

We had been together a long time. I walked down the street with a swollen belly, nursed and bathed you for three months, and thought about nothing but you since you attached yourself to my body and announced your existence.

Kelvin, we are all of them, you and I, and they are us. This ritual. This act. This separation. Our lives are recurring streams flowing into a river four hundred years old and this courtroom air stains our breathing, its thickness heavy upon us.

All of a sudden. All of a sudden. Without warning. No holding back. No retreat. No second thought. Forever. Here, the judge said. Take this pen. The gold-tipped fountain pen bled blue ink as I signed my name. The blue ink was dark, enpurpled, bloody, and if there is a balm in Gilead, I prayed, give it and if there is a healing do it. I walked out and stood on the courtroom stairs looking up. It had stopped snowing.

And if there is a balm, give it now, and if there is a healing, now please. I breathed in the fresh March air. We are in each other, May Anna, Kelvin, and I. From us, generations of life, and out of our excised past, the future. But what was I to do with the long years that stretched before me?

What can I do? But spin
And then spin
Again.

Out of me, my self, my Jacob's
ladder of God-Loyalty.
My Redemption.
My Heaven-House.

—Angela Jackson,
"The House of the Spider"

And only those who have chewed water
Know it has bones.

Virginia Hughes
(Aishah Rahman)

Providence, Rhode Island

Aishah Rahman's *Chewed Water,* from the weird, disturbing title, which drives you back to it several times to reach understanding of what she means . . . *chewed water!* The work, the process, the reason.

This is a book that wants to supply *whys* and inside that *hows.* Because for all the paradigmatic reality, rejected by the blind who lead the greedy as black sociopathological mythophrenia rather than the stuff that actual lives are made of, Ms. Rahman instead spreads out her earlier days of pain and frustration with emotional yet material precision, to confirm how lives are really shaped, like bullets against your wall.

Who Aishah Rahman is, became, despite or behind all that pain and edge-walking compulsion to become a singular dramatic voice from Afro-America, makes you re-see what we thought known, and touch the actual details of such a growing, and the uglier, more alienated, more daringly conscious path to herself.

We are also more clearly aware of the choices shaped by the day-to-day context of her suffering and subsequent near triumphant "true self-consciousness." The more complete environment of that pain, enlightenment, endarkenment, enhipment, if you will, how torture can be dug and willfully left behind.

What we know as serious with integrity is that that pain and ultimate comprehension of the world did not send her to the white-outorium of obscene profit where trendy thugs fashionably denounce Afro-America as registration of their honorary "profundity" and conditional uncoloredness.

Ms. Rahman carries her "baggage" as an indelible signature that she has paid her dues and a lotta other peepa's and is gonna talk about it, signify with it, bop us on our instruments of in dig nation, till she and all the we, understand, ourselves. And "What's going on."

Amiri Baraka